SURVIVAL:
Unite to Live

SURVIVAL:
Unite to Live

by Jim Bakker

New Leaf Press

P.O. BOX 1045, HARRISON, ARK. 72601

First Edition

Typesetting by Type-O-Graphics
Springfield, Mo. 65806

Library of Congress Catalog Card Number: 80-84504
International Standard Book Number: 0-89221-081-8

Dedication

To my wife Tammy who has stood with me through the valley and mountaintop experiences as I learned these difficult lessons of survival.

To my two terrific children, Tammy Sue and Jamie Charles.

And to all my faithful partners without whose help there would be no PTL.

Contents

Dedication v
Foreword ix
1 Who Is on the Lord's Side? 13
2 Ending Carnal Warfare 25
3 Known by Our Fruits 33
4 Renewing the Mind 53
5 The Acts of Love 63
6 Key Words for Survival 75
7 Give a Good Report 87
8 The Hour of the CHURCH 93
9 A Majority with God 103
10 The Lord Is on Our Side 113

Foreword

Although I am mentioned in Jim Bakker's book (as are others whom I count above myself) that is NOT why I'm writing this personal introduction. I am doing it because of Jim Bakker himself and his lovely wife Tammy.

Jim Bakker has suffered for Christ more than most men I know, and by his own honest admission says some of his sufferings are because he is a human being who makes mistakes and has shortcomings. And he openly shares his highs and lows, his accomplishments and failures. Despite the fact that Jim is a handsome man with a polished look, he is a man's man—gutsy above all we can imagine.

What drew me to Jim Bakker goes far beyond the splendid work he is doing for God but because he is doing it under public glare two hours a day on LIVE television—warts and all. He stands up and says what he is, what he believes, what he is doing—and when he reaches heartbreak hill, he breaks down and weeps like the rest of us mortals.

Most in his position would conceal their grief. But Jesus wept openly. Jeremiah said his head felt like a "fountain of tears." Peter, when he failed Jesus so miserably at the very hour Jesus needed a friend the most during His trial, went out and "wept bitterly," unmindful of who saw him.

Jim Bakker is for real—and anybody with an ounce of goodwill or a sense of appreciation for someone who tries can see and feel it.

I don't ordinarily write introductions, even for my best friends—just as I don't ask them to often write one for a book of mine. In the final analysis every child of God has to live "by faith" of his own. I am writing this one not because Jim called and asked. I am doing it because I see in Jim Bakker a 5′ 8″ guy who is doing the work of a 7 footer. He laughs, he cries, he speaks out, he goes for his topmost best; but when he hurts or misses the mark he feels God has set for him, he lets us see him exactly as he is. No phoniness. No effort to appear to feel what he does not. Like doing his "live" TV program with no time to edit out the "goofs." What you see is the way it is.

This world which wants men and women to be perfect, then tries to crucify them when they don't reach it—and surely would if they did reach perfection—needs to see . . . hear . . . and feel more Jim Bakkers. Yes, because he is becoming a strong Christian and spiritual leader in God's great work here on earth, a true pioneer in the most difficult field of all: being on LIVE television daily in the human arena of grime and blood and suffering of human beings. But also because whatever weaknesses Jim Bakker has he lets hang out for friend and foe alike to see.

Personally, I see a lot of our Master in Jim Bakker—and certainly in Tammy who stands for the Lord even when it is the toughest . . . and when she feels the deepest fears. They both tell me—and say it on the air—they want to be so much MORE like Jesus. They flatly say they haven't "arrived" and are not ashamed to admit it. Neither are they ashamed or intimidated by anybody—government, denomination, business, or any other part of the world we live in. I like that. I draw strength from it for my own shortcomings. Many times

I've actually felt the adrenaline flow, and I stand a little taller when I see these two young warriors standing up to what all of us would like to but sometimes are not willing to because of the fear of ridicule or failure.

Jim and Tammy, you are two who just won't give up. You won't quit. You will keep on keeping on when you are UP and when you are DOWN . . . because you are real, you are committed.

You have met Jesus and He is mastering your lives. He has shown you the race is long and hard, but you have burned your bridges and are striking your blows for the deliverance of the people by the Gospel of our Savior, Jesus Christ of Nazareth.

One more word . . .

The clouds are lifting! The dawn is breaking! It won't be long now! The Second Coming of the One Whose we are and Whom we serve is already brushing up against the devil and the opposers of God's anointed. Just one more tiny brush against Satan, and he will be through afflicting, tormenting, and destroying those for whom Jesus died and rose from the dead. And as you so often say that you have read the end of the *Book* and we win . . . well, we are winning, and winning will soon become not just a word but Christ Himself Who is even now looking over the battlements of heaven and saying, "Just keep your eyes on Me. You are doing fine. And the best is yet to come."

Your friend always,

Oral Roberts

1

Who Is
on the Lord's Side?

Mount St. Helens erupts, spewing ash and devastation over thousands of square miles, a Titan missile explodes on its pad in Arkansas, severe drought hits the mid-South and causes livestock deaths and crop failures, war and rumors of war abound in the oil-rich Middle East and other parts of the world, famine causes two-thirds of the world to go to bed hungry, the dollar shrinks, families fall apart, recession, hostages, Cuban refugees, hijackings, abortions, drugs, suicide . . . .

Catastrophes and problems encompass the globe, and mankind asks the question: How can we survive? For Christians, too, the question is just as important.

I believe that God has given me the answer—His formula for survival in these perilous times. And I want to share with you what the Church of Jesus Christ must do *now* to survive as we see these strange events sweeping the earth.

The children of Israel encountered strange sights, also. God was trying to get their attention just as He is trying to get the attention of the Church today.

Moses waited six days at the foot of Mount Sinai before hearing from God. On the seventh day all the children of Israel were awakened to the fury and awe of the sight of the glory of the Lord. It was like a devouring fire on the top of Sinai.

God began to speak to Moses and to give him instruction after instruction. Finally His mighty hand carved from the rock two tablets of stone on which He wrote the Royal Law, the Ten Commandments. All of this took time—as a matter of fact, forty days—to complete.

In the meantime, the children of Israel grew weary of waiting. They became restless and then impatient. Then their faith went. Finally, out went their belief in God. They decided that their God must be gone and that even their leader Moses must have perished with Him. In their own vain imaginations, they decided that they needed a new god to worship. So they went to Aaron, the priest and the brother of Moses, and told him to make them a golden god. Aaron gathered their jewelry and their gold and melted it and began to form a new god.

God saw what was happening. His wrath became hot and burning when He saw how in just forty days His chosen people were now bowing to a creature made with their own hands and their own gold. He said to Moses, "Lead them out; for I am going to consume all of them."

Moses pleaded their cause, and God withheld His wrath. The Scripture tells us of the evil He thought of doing to His people. Moses then went down the mountain with the two tablets of stone.

What a wonderful day of blessing this should have

been for the children of Israel. If only they had waited; if only they had trusted; if only they had prayed—to see the mighty hand of God.

How often today we take matters into our own hands rather than wait for the perfect will of God. The thirty-seventh Psalm tells us to wait patiently, and He will give us the desires of our hearts.

But, alas, this wasn't the case with the children of Israel. When Moses arrived at the base of the mountain, he saw what had happened, and he, too, became angry. He threw the tablets of stone down and broke them at the foot of the mountain.

Then he took their golden calf, their god, and ground it into powder. He threw the powder into the water and made them drink the water and, yes, their fashioned god.

Can you imagine what it was like for Moses to have been without food or shelter for forty days and to return from the most wonderful and awesome experience of his life only to see what he had seen before him in the camp?

I'm certain that as he stood at the gate of the camp his shout was not weak, but demanding and frightening. Many would die because they did not move when Moses shouted forth, *"Who is on the Lord's side? Let him come to me!"*

Then Moses stood still while the sons of Levi gathered themselves around him. And Moses commanded the men to take their swords and go into the camp and slay those who had not been faithful to God. Exodus 32:28 records that about three thousand men died that day.

The next day Moses cried out to the people, "You have sinned a great sin! Now I will go talk to the Lord to see if there is forgiveness."

Who is on the Lord's side? Who is on the Lord's side?

I believe that is the call that is still going out to the world and to God's people—the charismatic people and the non-charismatic people—all who are called by the name of the Lord God Almighty. God is saying today, "Who is on My side now?" I believe with all my heart that God is beginning to separate the sheep from the goats.

The tenth chapter of John expresses Christ's thought, "My sheep hear My voice, and they know Me. My sheep follow me. The sheep do My will."

It's easy to tell the difference between sheep and goats. Sheep are gentle. They're meek and they're lowly. They graze upon the good, fresh, green grass. The goats go around butting into everything they see, eating garbage. Their food basically consists of brush and brambles and the things no one else would want. Yes, there is a difference between sheep and goats.

For years now it seems as though God has more or less blinked His eye at sin. Everything seems to be muddled together. That which has distinguished Christians from the world can no longer be found. People no longer see Christians on the street or in the neighborhood and say, "That man is a Christian."

Churches have become popular. Religion has become popular. And in the midst of all of this, true Christianity and Jesus Christ have often become almost obliterated or, at least, overshadowed. We have not been able to really tell who was on the Lord's side and who wasn't.

But I want to tell you something. I believe the battle line has now been drawn. I believe that we as born-again, Christ-fearing Christians can no longer straddle the fence. God is calling us out, "Those who are on My side, come and step over the line and stand with Me now."

It makes me think of Martin Luther when he was

before the court. They were questioning him on his position on grace instead of works to obtain salvation. Finally he looked them square in the eye and said, "Here I stand." And that is what God is calling us to do now. "Here I stand." There is no middle ground. God wants us to be soldiers of the Cross equipped for battle, equipped for the war that is raging in these last days.

God wants us to be armed and ready to do battle. Ephesians 6:12 states, "For we wrestle not against flesh and blood, but against principalities, against powers, against the rulers of the darkness of this world, against spiritual wickedness in high places."

And the Scripture then directs the believer:

Wherefore take unto you the whole armour of God, that ye may be able to withstand in the evil day, and having done all, to stand. Stand, therefore, having your loins girt about with the truth, and having on the breastplate of righteousness, and your feet shod with the preparation of the gospel of peace. Above all, taking the shield of faith, wherewith ye shall be able to quench all the fiery darts of the wicked. And take the helmet of salvation, and the sword of the Spirit, which is the word of God: praying always with all prayer and supplication in the Spirit, and watching thereunto with all perseverance and supplication for all saints.

Yes, when we're equipped with the armor of God, we can defeat the enemy. The battle lines have been drawn. We can see that it's Satan (even his men in "high places") warring against God's children.

Yes, the battle lines are drawn between good and evil, between right and wrong, between God and Satan, yes, between the sheep and the goats. The battle cry has been sounded.

When the Full Gospel Businessmen International convention was held recently in Los Angeles, Oral Roberts gave one of the most powerful messages that I've ever heard. He came and knelt and gave forth the battle cry. He cried for Christians to man their battle stations and to go forward in the name of Jesus.

We are now in an era of evangelism, a new era of dedication, a new era for Christianity. From now on, I believe, it's "Onward Christian Solders, Marching As to War." And if you, my friend, do not believe we're in warfare, you've been living in a make-believe world. We are in battle. We're in a battle now to the end, to the final hour. Praise God, we know we are going to win, for the battle is the Lord's.

Our weapons are not carnal. God is our source, and we have secret weapons in Jesus that this old world knows nothing of.

Satan, at this present time, is bringing out all his artillery against the Church of Jesus Christ. But he doesn't know and understand that great Invisible Shield around us, and that no weapon formed against us is going to prosper.

Recently, as I was meditating, the Lord spoke to me a word of prophecy, and this is what He said, "Some of you evangelists will have your lives threatened, and some of you they will even try to assassinate. But I want you to know that not one is going to be harmed. For I say again, according to my Word, that no weapon formed against you is going to prosper."

Satan knows that his days are limited. He knows the hour of his doom is upon him. He's scared. Even the political forces are afraid of the Church of Jesus Christ today. Thank God that we do not have to fight with carnal weapons!

In 2 Corinthians 10:3-5 we read, "For though we walk in the flesh, we do not war after the flesh: (For the weapons of our warfare are not carnal, but mighty through God to the pulling down of strongholds;) casting down imaginations, and every high thing that exalteth itself against the knowledge of God, and bringing into captivity every thought to the obedience of Christ."

There is an attack on the Church today like never before. I talk with pastors who are trying to build churches, and because of so many of the ordinances that have been passed in the United States of America, in places it's almost impossible to build a church.

You may ask, "How can they stop a church?" Simple. They just won't give you a driveway permit. You can't park cars if you can't get them in. They might not give you a sewer permit. It's hard to have a church when you have regulations almost forbidding you to have bathrooms.

"In America," you might ask, "this is happening?" Yes. In America. And we had better wake up. It is so very subtle that we hardly are aware that it is happening.

For years we have been taught to sit back and do nothing and say nothing—that we should be meek and mild and let the systems of the world run roughshod over us. But I've got news for America. If the Christians in Germany would have stood up, Hitler would never have gotten into power. But the church became a religion of brick and mortar and massive buildings and not a vibrant relationship with a living Christ. And that's why a madman got into power. If good men do nothing, sin will reign; evil will reign.

Men of integrity have been blasphemed in America. It seems today it's more popular to be a sinner than a saint. Recently in North Carolina they brought out the bands and had a parade to welcome a new brewery into the state. But if a man like Oral Roberts wants to build the world's largest medical center, they want to tar and feather him. They don't want to give him building permits. They don't want this to happen, and they don't want that to happen. And they almost succeeded. But, praise God, just the other day I saw him turn the last bolt into place on the superstructure.

Billy Graham (whom I respect so deeply and who, I believe, is the prophet of God for this generation in calling men to repentance) is the John the Baptist of this generation, crying out, "Repent or perish!" The news media has tried to smear him over a secret fund that he is supposed to have. Isn't it strange that the very newspaper that dug up that story has a document in its own files, according to one of its own reporters, that says that two years earlier the newspaper had public knowledge about that so called "secret fund."

Isn't it something when a man like Rex Humbard, with over thirty years in the ministry, is accused of such hideous things that have been in the media lately. I happen to know Rex and Maude Aimee very well, and I know the truth about that so-called scandal. And it's a lie. Very few bother to go all the way to find out that the church was paying Rex Humbard back the money the church owed him when he had mortgaged his own house to keep his church from going under a few years ago. They didn't bother to research far enough to find that the church was just paying Rex Humbard back the money that they owed him.

The SEC came into Rex Humbard's ministry. One of those great government officials pounded his fist on the table and said, "You Christians have had your day. Well, I'm telling you it's over!"

They did the same thing to Revival Fires. The agents of the U.S. government came in and said, "We've got forty of you evangelical groups, and you're through! We're going to close you all down!" But they have not succeeded in closing one of our ministries down. Why? No weapon that is formed against us is going to prosper.

Oral Roberts has one of the greatest concepts of healing of any man of this generation. The medical center and the healing teams are perhaps the most awesome and challenging missionary endeavors that I've ever heard of in my lifetime. Oral has a vision to send teams around the world—doctors, nurses, ministers, and professional people—all with the goal of bringing Christ to the nations. Oral has a single-minded vision: to win the world to Jesus Christ in the next few years. His God is not known for thinking small.

God told him to build a medical center bigger than any other that man has ever built. And the world (Satan) just simply cannot handle it. Their egos have been hurt. They have been intimidated. They have been challenged with the reality of a living Saviour, Jesus Christ. But God is alive and active and tearing down demonic strongholds.

They used to call us "old time pentecostal holy rollers." And many today are even calling the charismatics "holy rollers." They refer to us in the same way the Jews referred to Jesus—as "Joseph's boy." The Jews said, "It's just Jesus. Isn't He one of Joseph's kids? What good can come out of Nazareth? Who can heal? Who can do this? Who can do that?"

They didn't worry about us much as long we just preached. As a matter of fact, they didn't care if we just preached that God was a healer, or that God was our provider, or that Jesus was our baptizer in the Holy Spirit, or that God would give us prosperity.

At the time that the baptism of the Holy Spirit first emerged in this century, most of the evangelists were preaching in tents or cowsheds or storefront buildings. Most of the high and mighty just chuckled under their breath, ". . . Crazy, disallusioned people—if we ignore it, it will go away like the measles or mumps or any other irritant."

But one thing they didn't count on was the prophecy of Joel. In Joel 2:28-30 God says, "And it shall come to pass afterward, that I will pour out my spirit upon all flesh; and your sons and your daughters shall prophesy, your old men shall dream dreams, your young men shall see visions: and also upon the servants and upon the handmaids in those days will I pour out my spirit. And I will show wonders in the heavens and in the earth, blood, and fire, and pillars of smoke."

Today we are seeing that vision coming to pass. We are seeing the Spirit of God like a blanket covering the entire world. The baptism of the Holy Spirit is reaching into the old-line denominational churches. It has swept across the Catholic church, and today it is not unusual at all to see nuns in their meetings standing with their hands uplifted, praising Jesus.

Several years ago it was such wonderful news to hear that in Minneapolis at the Lutheran charismatic convention that a Lutheran pastor and a Catholic priest asked each other for forgiveness because of their bitterness toward each other's faith. Because of what the Spirit of God had done, they knelt before each other and in humility washed each other's feet. You see, when we know Jesus Christ as our personal Saviour, and we realize that the Word of God is infallible and that the blood of Jesus is the only source for our atonement and that He's coming again in glory, we can have fellowship one with another.

Mount St. Helens has been an interesting thing to observe. For we see devastation and destruction and pillars of smoke ascending thousands of feet into the air and the ash blanket covering a large portion of the United States. Earth tremors and quakes and floods and drought and plagues. Starvation. Yes, we're living in those days that Joel described.

With the sweep of the Holy Spirit across the land, our hearts are growing strong. Faith is increasing, and therefore God's children are marching. Today we're building the world's largest medical centers, and it scares the enemies of Christ. We're building cathedrals that hold thousands. And it frightens them. We're building buildings and taking over the airways. And it scares them.

The forces of Satan are drawing together to make a last stand against the cause of Christ. But God's Spirit is raising up a mighty standard to defeat Satan, and that standard is the Church. If the Church is going to defeat Satan, if the Church is going to survive the greatest attack of the ages, then the Church must unite—She must unite to live!!

2
Ending
Carnal Warfare

When radio first came on the scene, Christians debated whether or not it was of God because of Ephesians 2:2 which states, "Wherein in time past ye walked according to the course of this world, according to the prince of the power of the air, the spirit that now worketh in the children of disobedience." Debate lasted for months and years, until finally radio station WMBI at Moody Bible Institute came on the airways. I believe this was the first Christian radio station.

Then television came along. And Christians, for the most part, were convinced that it was from the pit of hell. But, praise God, today we are saying with the Apostle Paul, "I can do all things through Christ which strengtheneth me."

We have dared to be conquerors. We have dared to move the mountain. We have dared to shout it from the housetops. We have dared to put seed faith to the test. We have dared to expect a hundredfold for that which we have given. And God has honored His Word. We are marching.

Today many of the worldly authorities are scared. Many of the big corporations are trembling. Why? Because Christianity and Christians are marching. We are finally out front instead of last. We are finally the head instead of the tail. For so long they've been used to being the head and just ignoring us. Now they don't know what to do with us.

When satellites became commercially available, PTL was among the first to invest in this area—only to be followed by some of the major corporations of the country. We started our programming in April of 1978, and now more than 100 hours of Christian ministry television programs are aired free of charge every week over the network. We now have about 223 broadcast affiliates and 296 cable stations. Imagine the people we can reach for Christ.

Through the satellite delivery system, cable systems in every state are able to offer their subscribers twenty-four hours of the finest in Christian programming every day.

Here at PTL we have been offered money for our station and our satellite network time and time again. The world wants to get our transponder.

If PTL wanted to sell out to the world right now, we could pay every bill that PTL has and rebuild everything that has been built all over again and perhaps even have money left over. I wish I could share with you who has been phoning our corporate offices trying to buy our network. It must have been real humbling for the big businessmen who are not used to associating with PTL. And I humbly thank Jesus that we finally have something that they want.

The biggest newspapers in America have called, wanting to buy our network. Some of the world's largest conglomerates have called, wanting to buy our network. They would pay us literally millions upon millions of dollars because we have it. And they don't realize, "We ain't givin' it up!" The prince of the power of the air is defeated, and he's going down for the last time. The Scriptures tell us that this would happen. And now, I believe, the day is soon coming that Satan will be consigned to hell.

There are some things in life that money cannot buy. I'm afraid that too many people of the world—even as was true of the children of Israel while Moses was in the mountain—have made gold their god. And therefore they think God can be overcome and discredited with gold.

The world cannot understand the Body of Jesus Christ because, for the most part, all they understand is dollars and dollars and dollars. And they think all of us have a dollar motive in mind. They never stop to contemplate that our hearts pant after God and that our supreme objective in life is to win souls to Jesus Christ. They simply do not understand the worth of an eternal—an eternal—soul.

Now that we are preaching to our nation by live satellite, there isn't enough money in the world to buy that satellite from PTL. Our dividend is not dollars, it's souls. We are placing souls into the bank of Heaven, and that's where our dollars and cents are. That's where our profit lies—in souls. Souls, souls, souls.

What's going to happen when this enemy comes in on us? No matter what form Satan takes, whether it's government intervention or whatever, God tells us in 2 Corinthians 10:45 that He will take care of every high thing that exalts itself against the knowledge of God. Today we see this all over the world. There are those who think they are mightier than God. As a result, they don't want us on the airways because they don't want us giving out the knowledge of God. But I pity these, for their downfall is certain. You see, it's been promised by God Almighty Himself.

The world has standard operating procedures for their negotiations, but they find it very hard to deal with all of us religious "fanatics." For, you see, we don't pay bribes to build our buildings. That's a switch, isn't it? And the world knows what I'm talking about. There are a lot of places where if you don't pay bribes, you don't get anything. It has become a lifestyle. Hardly a day goes by that you can't pick up the paper and read of a major scandal by a major corporation dealing under the table.

Believe it or not, I'm still operating under a temporary occupancy for my studio that was built over four years ago in Charlotte, North Carolina. And isn't it strange that a former state senator has the same equipment and the same lighting that I have in his studio which was built the same time as mine. He has an occupancy permit and I don't. I have been told time and time again, "Why don't you pay a few bribes here and there, Bakker, and someone will get it through for you." No way. No way will I ever bow my knee to Baal. I'm not of his kingdom. My weapons are not carnal.

Pay attention now to what I'm saying, friend. This warfare must not be directed toward the Body of Christ. Our warfare must never be directed against each other. Pay attention to what Jesus has to say about this and listen to Him very carefully. It states in Matthew 12:25, "And Jesus knew their thoughts, and said unto them,

Every kingdom divided against itself is brought to desolation; and every city or house divided against itself shall not stand."

We need each other. Yes, we need each other. It is time that we realize that we must stop wounding and destroying one another and realize what army we're in and who our enemy is. It is Satan and all of his cohorts.

Again I refer to Ephesians 6:12. And we must allow the Scripture to penetrate our hearts. Pray and ask God that the Scripture might live in our hearts—somehow go from our minds to our hearts. For it is the fact of the Word being hidden in our hearts that keeps us from sin. The Scripture tells us over and over that our lips honor Him but our hearts do not. Man looks on the outward appearance, but God looks on the heart.

Ephesians 6:12 states, "We wrestle not against flesh and blood." We don't wrestle against each other. The battle is not between charismatics and non-charismatics. The battle is not between the Assembly of God and the Baptists. It is not between the Catholics and the Protestants. The battle is not against whether we baptize by immersion, pouring, or sprinkling. The battle is not against whether we believe Jesus is coming pre-, mid-, or post-tribulation. But the battle is "against principalities, against powers, against the rulers of the darkness of this world, against spiritual wickedness in high places."

It is Satan. He is our common enemy. He is so clever that he gets us fighting against each other, and then his work can flourish.

James 4:7 tells us that if we *submit* to God and resist the devil that he will flee from us. But I'm afraid we're so busy destroying each other, that we forget to submit to God. And Satan has his heyday.

Several years ago I asked God how we would all survive. How were we going to survive if all the shortages came upon us? How would we survive economic setbacks? And God, as He always does, spoke to my heart and gave me a precious Scripture, Hebrews 10:25, "Not forsaking the assembling of ourselves together, as the manner of some is; but exhorting one another: and so much the more, as ye see the day approaching."

We need each other. Don't despise your local church. Don't despise the local assembly. Get into local groups and bodies. Become involved with what God is doing in your city. And if nothing is happening in your city, have the faith to make it happen, and it will.

The world is looking to see love in Christians. They're looking for the fulfillment of Jesus' words in John 13:35, "By this shall all men know that ye are my disciples, if ye have love one to another."

First Corinthians 12:26 says, "And whether one member suffers, all the members suffer with it; or one member be honoured, all the members rejoice with it."

I have a career army man on my staff who serves as my aide. And I asked him the other day, "What would happen if one of the generals was captured?"

And he said, "Every man and woman in the army, every power, every force, everything known to that army would be put into gear and into service. They would work together to rescue their general."

I hope that would be true of us today. But what do we do with born-again Christians? What do we do in the Body of Christ when one of our generals is shot down? What do we do when one is wounded? What do we do when one has fallen in battle? Do we go over to them and grind our heels into their faces, leave them alone, spit at them, or gossip about them? Do we glory in their death? I'm afraid some of us do.

When Rex Humbard is having a problem, that's Jim Bakker's problem. That's Oral Roberts' problem. That's Billy Graham's problem. That's Jerry Falwell's problem. That's Pat Robertson's problem. And likewise, when Oral Roberts is having a problem, that's Billy Graham's, Pat Robertson's, and Rex Humbard's problem. And when General Billy Graham is having his problem, that likewise is all of Christendom's problem. When Pat Robertson is having a battle, that is our battle. When Jim Bakker is having a problem and is called before the government, that is Christianity being called before the government. That is the Body of Christ's problem.

Do you realize what happens when an army begins to shoot at itself? It loses and goes down in defeat.

Too often we would rather gossip than love. We would rather judge than give the benefit of the doubt. Love covers a multitude of sins, but hate and discord spread it. We must no longer tolerate that spirit—the usurping spirit that says, "If that preacher comes down, I'll go up." That's not true. If one of the brethren falls, we all fall.

When the floodtide of God's blessing comes in, and the water of His blessing rises, all the ducks in the pond go up with it. But when drought is upon the pond and the water level goes down, all the ducks go down with it. United we win. Divided we simply will destroy ourselves.

One of my pet peeves is that group of people that seems to be everywhere and in every church. They are always trying to unseat a pastor, unseat a deacon, tear down a ministry, come against founders of Christian organizations, etc. These are always the "super spiritual" people who make you very much aware that there is no sin in their life. They "nitpick" at every tiny error that the pastor, his wife, or anybody else makes. Believe me, you can see them coming a mile away. When I see these self-righteous people, I want to run in the other direction.

It's interesting how these people can ignore their own sins and lash out as vicious as cobras against their brother, trying to bring him down. If we could only realize that the world is watching. Their reaction is, "If that is Christianity, I don't want any part of it." And what a strong judgment is going to come against those who destroy the work of God.

I would like to challenge these people that are so super spiritual. Why don't they pray and let God move that man and bring him unto repentance instead of getting so carnal and ripping up the Church of Jesus Christ. *Either you believe the Book, the Word of God, or you don't.* Either it works or it doesn't. We have got to stop playing God and trying to manipulate situations, organizations, churches, and people, or we will not survive.

3

Known
by Our Fruits

It is time that we stop taking the ministry and the work of God and putting it into our own hands, trying to elevate our own positions by tearing down the positions of others. If we believe the Word of God, then we'll believe Psalm 75:6-7, "For promotion cometh neither from the east, nor from the west, nor from the south. But God is the judge: he putteth down one, and setteth up another."

David, who was to become the king of Israel, knew better than to harm one of God's anointed. First Samuel 26 gives the account of David's opportunity to kill King Saul, who was actively trying to kill David.

David happened to come upon King Saul and some of his men while they were sleeping, and David could have done anything he wanted to do to them. Abashai, one of David's soldiers, saw King Saul sleeping on the ground and said to David, "God hath delivered thine enemy into thine hand this day: now therefore let me smite him, I pray thee, with the spear even to the earth at once, and I will not smite him the second time.''

David quickly responded, "Destroy him not: for who can stretch forth his hand against the Lord's anointed, and be guiltless? As the Lord liveth, the Lord shall smite him; or his day shall come to die; or he shall descend into battle, and perish. The Lord forbid that I should stretch forth mine hand against the Lord's anointed.''

David had the opportunity to destroy someone who was against him, and he had just cause. But David knew God's way was better! If David would have destroyed King Saul, he would have set a precedent and probably would have been killed himself when he became king.

I believe that the day is here when we had better start being careful, and I mean *very* careful. Ananias and Sapphira tried to play a little game with the work of God, and they were stricken dead. I want to share something with you. I believe that we are in the New Testament Church Age like we have never been before. I want you to realize that the book hasn't been closed on the day of Ananias and Sapphira.

Recently God talked to me about this. We are not going to get by any longer with tearing down His Body as we have for the last few years. God is not going to endure it any longer. The hour is upon us when, I believe, He is going to deal harshly with those of us who tear apart the Body of Jesus Christ, telling lies, perverting stories, and trying to bring another brother down.

I've had so many people try to take over the ministry here at PTL over the years. It has happened so often that I am almost paranoid when hiring an executive. There always seems to be one who thinks he can buy the gifts of God just as Simon tried in Acts 8. The world has many Simons.

I can simply tell you that if God has called you to a ministry, then start your own. And if indeed it is the call of God, He'll bless it; if it isn't, He won't.

Even though some of the preachers and evangelists that you know might not be much, and to you they might be just one of "Joseph's boys," remember he's still God's anointed. All Christians who are doing the will of God are under the anointing of God. If you think you're a better preacher than your pastor, then go build a church of your own. But don't rip up his church.

The story of Haman and Mordecai is a classic example of the saying in Scripture, "Touch not God's anointed." In the Book of Esther, we find Esther, who was a Jewess, coming before King Ahasuerus. She received favor in his sight and was made queen. She obeyed her uncle Mordecai's command that she tell no one that she was a Jewess.

A man by the name of Haman came into prominence in the kingdom and commanded that all bow before him. But Mordecai refused.

When Haman realized that Mordecai would not bow because of his faith, he decided to destroy all the Jews in the land.

Haman went to the king and told him that he should get rid of all the Jews in the land, for they were going to ruin and overthrow his kingdom. The king made a decree that they should hunt out, destroy, and kill all the Jews—both young and old, little children, and women—in one day, and he placed his seal on the decree.

When Mordecai heard this, he tore his clothes and put on sackcloth with ashes and lamented before the king's gate.

This decree meant that Esther would also have to be

killed, for she too was a Jew.

Esther told her uncle Mordecai to gather all the Jews together and fast and pray for three days. She then put on royal apparel and stood before the king. When King Ahasuerus saw her, she obtained favor in his sight, and he bid her to come forward.

As she touched the top of his sceptre, the king said, "What do you want, Esther? I'll give it to you—even up to half of the kingdom." She requested that the king and Haman come to a banquet she'd prepared for them. Of course the king bade Haman to come.

When that banquet was over, she requested they come again the second day. Haman was delighted that Esther had only requested the king and himself to come to the table. This was unheard of. Yet, Haman said, "Even all this glory doesn't do me much good when I see Mordecai sitting outside of the gate refusing to bow before me."

Haman's wife encouraged him to build the gallows and speak to the king so that Mordecai could be hanged.

The king realized that Mordecai, who had once saved the king's life, had not been rewarded and wanted to reward him. At the same time Haman came before the king to ask for the life of Mordecai.

Before Haman could speak, the king asked him, "What should I do with a man that I want to honor?"

Haman thought in his heart, "The king must be referring to me," and he said, "Give the man royal apparel that the king has used and a horse that the king has ridden upon, and set the royal crown upon his head."

The king said to Haman, "Make haste and take the apparel and the horse and all you have said and do to Mordecai the Jew that sits at the king's gate. Let nothing fail of all that you have spoken."

Haman had no choice but to obey the king.

The next day Haman and the king were to again appear at the banquet planned by Esther.

The king again asked Esther's petition, and she said to the king, "Let me have my life and my people, for we have been sold. My people are to be destroyed, to be slain, and to perish."

Then the king said unto Esther, "Who's he and where is he who would dare do this to my queen?"

Esther said, "It is Haman."

Then the king, arising from the table, went to the palace garden, and Haman stood up to make a request for his life to Esther, the queen, because he saw that the king was all set to punish him.

Haman had fallen on Queen Esther's bed as he was pleading with her, and when the king saw this, he was angrier than ever. Without any more questions the king said, "Hang Haman on the gallows that he has prepared for Mordecai."

Haman, with all of his cunning—trying to destroy God's anointed—died on the very gallows that he had prepared for Mordecai.

That is a severe warning for us today that we likewise touch not the anointed ones of God. For we like Haman will be caught and snared in our own traps.

I've discovered that most of man's problems really stem from the root of covetousness and jealousy. And of course we know that jealousy is one of the basic roots from which all evil comes. And the Scripture simply tells us that we should always "prefer one another."

We, as brothers and sisters, can do more to destroy each other than all the world put together. Do you want to know who tried to remove me from PTL? It was my own brethren—some of those who were under my employ. Do you want to know who tried to pass a law in our state to license religious organizations so that PTL couldn't grow and must be regulated by various controls? It was a religious group, and if I named them, you would fall over in a faint because a major denomination was behind it. And yet I know that behind that lies the pushiness and the destructive power of Satan.

The greatest opposition to the Church is coming from within the so-called body. And yet I don't believe they're all really in the Body. I believe we have "wolves in sheep's clothing." Just because they walk under the Christian flag doesn't mean they are true believers. Let's remember, "By their fruits ye shall know them."

Abraham Lincoln, in one of his great speeches, made the statement concerning America that we don't have to fear those from without our shores, but we have to be aware of the rot and decay from within. If America falls, it will be from decay from within and not from without.

And I truly believe that the same is true of the Church. Most of the decay, most of the arguments, fights, and battles are from within, not from without.

I would like to share with you a few verses from Proverbs 6:16-19. As you read these verses, I want you to keep your mind open.

These six things doth the Lord hate: yea, seven are an abomination unto him: a proud look, a lying tongue, and hands that shed innocent blood, an heart that deviseth wicked imaginations, feet that be swift in running to mischief, a false witness that speaketh lies, and he that soweth discord among brethren.

It is sad, but I must say that in the last two years I have found more Christians lying and being haughty or proud that they have this or they've done that or etc., etc. And I wonder very strongly if they are indeed Christians. I'm sorry, but lying and the haughty look are the fruits of the flesh, not the fruits of the Spirit of the Living Christ.

The Scripture tells us simply that liars will not enter Heaven. You might add here, "I'm a salesman; I have to lie." No you don't. There is never an instance that any man has got to lie. Yet, there are men who have gotten into such a lifestyle of lying that they wouldn't know the truth if it hit them between the eyes.

We need to get back to the basic simplicity of the Word of God; we need to get back to the realization of the three mighty words, "Thou shalt not;" we need to get back to kindergarten and start all over again with the basics. We need to be careful of the "silly women" syndrome (2 Tim. 3:6) that is eating away at the charismatic movement.

I have seen women (and men too, I might add) come to my ministry and stay with me six months to a year. Then they move on to Oral Roberts' ministry and then to Gerald Derstine's, etc., etc. They're charismatic groupies. They come around saying, "I've been down to so-and-so, and it's not what it's cracked up to be." And, "Brother So-and-So—he isn't a real man of God, because my 'sick cat' was dying and he wouldn't come and pray for it."

Oh, dear God, the lies, the lies, the lies that are told in Christendom today. My friends, your greatest friend in the world is truth. Don't ever become associated with a witness that is speaking lies. It will kill you.

Recently, a national news program did a little segment on Oral Roberts. The half-truths that came across on that program were appalling. For example, they cut up

Oral Roberts' brother's statement so that it came out a lie. Oral's brother said, "I've never seen Oral heal anyone, but I've seen God through Oral heal many people." And that was a wonderful statement. But when they chopped it in two, it merely came out with him saying, "I've never seen Oral heal anyone." Period. That sounds mighty strange coming from the brother of Oral Roberts. Therefore, it put Oral down, and that is not at all what Oral's brother intended. It was a false witness. I want to say to you men who are on that broadcast, God hated that.

I think perhaps the worst in this list from Proverbs 6 would be those who sow discord among the brethren, constantly stirring to keep people in agony and frustration and confusion. A lot of people are convinced that if we could get other people cleaned up, we'd have a perfect Church. I suppose that is true. But one thing we have failed to realize is that we can't clean anybody up. Only the Spirit of God can cleanse and purify. It would be wonderful if all the staff members, starting with myself, could be absolutely without fault. But I know and you know that every one of us has a problem of one sort or another that the Spirit of God is dealing with.

Yes, I believe there's not one exception, and if you say you don't, then you really have a problem. Everyone of us has to battle with something. We either have to battle with our money problems or temper or maybe lust. All of us have a "thorn in the flesh."

Yet, in spite of all this, we seem to always be trying to find and expose every sin we can find in a brother while we ignore our own—or, at least, keep it hidden. But the Scripture tells us that our sins will find us out.

It seems that so much of the conversation that transpires today is gossip, gossip, gossip. "Did you know that so-and-so smokes? Did you know that so-and-so did this? Did you know that so-and-so is thinking about leaving his wife? Did you know that I think I saw so-and-so here or so-and-so doing this?" And we yak and yak and yak.

And then there are those who say, "If this man didn't come to our church, we'd be so much better off. If this one didn't come . . . . If we could just get her out of our sewing circle, it would be so much better. It's those rotten teenagers that spoil our church."

I remember when I was a young teen, seeking desperately to walk with the Lord. I had just gotten a job as a young rock 'n roll disc jockey. My church, or at least some in the church, wanted to throw me out because I wasn't a good testimony and I wasn't fit to associate with the church kids anymore. But thank God, there were some who were sensitive enough to the Spirit of God to love me over this "hassle" in my life. When Jim Bakker came to church, some of those old saints threw their arms around me and prayed for me. They continued to love me, and because of that I stayed true to God. I often wonder what would have happened if they had thrown me out. I would still probably be out in the world somewhere.

It is time we realize that the local church is not a club for perfect people. The local church certainly should be an emergency room for sick souls that need help—the lame, the halt, the troubled, the marriages that are breaking up—and the church should be pouring in the wine and the oil, the kind that restores the soul.

If you want to have victory in your life, victory in your church, victory in your home, and if you want strife to go out, follow Proverbs 26:20: "Where no wood is, there the fire goeth out: so where there is no talebearer, the strife ceaseth."

Many of us constantly try to blame the unsaved for many of our problems. No. It's often the hypocrite Christian, the gossip that bears the tales, that causes the division. If you want revival in your church, then shut your mouth. Put your tongue on the altar. Stop gossiping, stop slandering, stop talebearing. Some of you might even say at this point, "But what I say is true." Whether it's true or not, it's still talebearing, and it causes strife in the Body of Jesus Christ.

"Well," some people might add, "I heard that Oral Roberts or Billy Graham or Jim Bakker . . . you know, the paper said this or the paper said that. And, you know, where there's smoke there's a fire." And you see that gleam in their eye. What they say is not necessarily so. You didn't get that "where there's smoke there's fire" out of the Scripture. I would like to add, where there's smoke there's big, fat, gossiping talebearers. That's what it is and no more.

Then many add, "Well, there's a little truth to every rumor." That also isn't out of the Bible, and it isn't true. Either we're going to believe the Bible or we're not going to believe the Bible. Either we're going to live according to the teachings of Jesus Christ or we're not. Whose side are you on?

If anything today is an abomination to God, it is when people destroy the Body of Jesus Christ. It is the false witness and he that sows discord amongst the brethern. Proverbs 10:12 tells us, "Hatred stirreth up strifes: but love covereth all sins." Proverbs is such a book of wisdom for everyday living. If we want to know how to walk with God and run our businesses and our homes, we should heed the words of Proverbs.

We also read in Proverbs 11:13, "A talebearer

revealeth secrets: but he that is of a faithful spirit concealeth the matter." So, if you want to prove to anyone that you are spiritual, you won't spread gossip and slander and call on the phone and tell this one or that one, "Have you heard this or have you heard that?" You will simply keep it within you and go to your closet and pray.

I believe the era of the charismatic "cocktail party" is over—running from tingle to tingle and jingle to jingle. Second Timothy 4:3-4 speaks, "For the time will come when they will not endure sound doctrine; but after their own lusts shall they heap to themselves teachers, having itching ears; and they shall turn away their ears from the truth, and shall be turned unto fables."

We need to grow up and get away from the tinkling cymbals and sounding brass. We need to get into the Word of God, search it out, and let it speak to us. We need to hear how the Holy Spirit would teach us. We need to be grounded in the Word and stop looking for another teacher or another preacher to tickle our fancy and give us something that would only stir us up for the moment before going on to the next thing.

Over the years I've seen the masses go from one teaching to another—from inner healing to demons, from demons to faith, from faith to prosperity, then to the doctrine of angels, then back to shepherdship and discipleship, and on and on like the tide coming in and out. Even though there are truths in all of these teachings, we need to keep our lives in balance; we need to keep our doctrine in balance; we need to keep our faith in balance. For error is simply truth out of focus.

We're admonished in Hebrews 5:12-14, "For when for the time ye ought to be teachers, ye have need that one teach you again which be the first principles of the oracles of God; and are become such as have need of milk, and not of strong meat. For every one that useth milk is unskillful in the word of righteousness: for he is a babe. But strong meat belongeth to them that are of full age, even those who by reason of use have their senses exercised to discern both good and evil.''

Over and over again I've seen the lack of the knowledge of the Word of God. People are misquoting the Word, and it becomes very evident that many are looking for a thrill and not a *foundation*. I see this as one of the greatest dangers that we have in the charismatic movement today: the lack of knowledge of the Word. There are those who speak very loudly and profoundly that "I'm standing on the Word." But in a short time you discover that they were standing on an isolated Bible verse taken out of context, or they're quoting something out of context. They really don't know whereof they speak.

The Psalmist tell us in Psalm 119:11, "Thy Word have I hid in mine heart, that I might not sin against thee." And, people, if we want to be victorious in our walk with Jesus Christ, we certainly need to be grounded in the Word of God.

We have come to the end of the hallelujah parties. The charismatic honeymoon is over. And now it is time that we man our battle stations.

If a soldier in the army was without discipline and did as he pleased while the war was raging and if he decided he wouldn't go to the front lines but instead would say to himself, "I think I will go to town today," or, "I'll do this," or, "I don't want to work in the mess hall today," it wouldn't be long until he would be court martialed. He would be out of the good graces of the army.

Yet, that's the way most of the charismatics have

been. We've been nothing more than charismatic grasshoppers, hopping from here to there—this meeting or that meeting, this man or that man, this woman or that woman. How little time we are spending before the throne of grace and in the Word of God. We need to be still, stay put, and let our roots grow deep in the Word so that we might bloom and bear fruit.

I'm amazed at how many times God has changed His mind for some people. And yet we hear Jesus speak in Luke 9:62, "No man, having put his hand to the plough, and looking back, is fit for the kingdom of God." Either Jesus Christ said that or He didn't say it.

The day has come when we must stand firm. Now is the time when we should be armed with the full power of God. Now is the time to realize that we are in a battle to the end. We have not come through this great charismatic movement of teaching and learning, of ministering in the gifts of the Spirit, just to have another tingle or to have another great glory session.

God has prepared a mighty army to go forth and take the world for Jesus Christ in these last hours. We must see that sound doctrine of the Word is well implanted in our minds and in our hearts. We must also be aware of false teachers and prophets who come to us in sheep's clothing but inwardly are raging wolves. We shall know them by their fruits.

Matthew 7:15-20 says,

Beware of false prophets, which come to you in sheep's clothing, but inwardly they are ravening wolves. *Ye shall know them by their fruits.* Do men gather grapes of thorns, or figs of thistles? Even so every good tree bringeth forth good fruit; but a corrupt tree bringeth forth evil fruit. A good tree cannot bring forth evil fruit, neither can a corrupt tree bring forth good fruit. Every tree that bringeth not forth good fruit is hewn down, and cast into the fire. Wherefore by their fruits ye shall know them.

Many might ask the question, "Then how are we going to judge—how are we going to cast the evil out of our assemblies?" We are going to fruit inspect. Yes, we must judge people by their fruits and not by their faults. And before we can judge other people's fruits, we must examine our own motives. I have seen too many people hide their own judging attitudes behind the cover of fruit inspecting.

Ask yourself, "What has Billy Graham done for the cause of Christ? What are his fruits? How many people have come to the Lord because of his life?" Your answer would be obvious. He has stayed true to the Word of God. He has stayed true to Jesus Christ. And thousands will be in Heaven because of his testimony.

What has Rex Humbard done? In Brazil alone recently the crowds were probably some of the largest in the history of world evangelism.

What has Oral Roberts done? Built one of the finest Christian universities the world has ever known.

By their fruits ye shall know them. No one even needs to be bright to figure out who the men of God are these days. Yes, there are a lot of people, I'm afraid, speaking of how great they are, what they can do, the great amount of faith they have, and this and that, and yet, simply ask yourself, "What kind of fruits are they bearing?"

It is time that we begin to recognize who the Body of Jesus Christ is and begin preparing now for the kingdom of God. If you are born-again, you have already been born into this great kingdom. Even if you do not speak in tongues or prophesy or have words of knowledge, if you have been born-again through the blood of Jesus Christ, you are in the family of God. You are my brother or my sister, and someday we are going to join hands together and go up in the rapture together to meet Jesus and be with God.

I believe God is telling us to embrace all born-again Christians all over the world, to enlarge the Body of Christ into the greatest love movement that has ever been. He is calling us to reach out as the Body of Christ comes together. Let's face it, Jesus is coming for one Bride, not thousands of brides.

I have learned one thing. When I love people, they want what I have. And it's not long until they are speaking in a language known only to Him.

Putting people down or setting yourself up or judging or condemning will never lead anyone into this great movement of the Spirit of God. We must let go of the word *hate*. The only one you can or dare to hate is the devil. Never try to vindicate yourself, for that is a part of talebearing. For Romans 12:19 says, "Vengeance is mine; I will repay, saith the Lord." You don't ever have to be the other person's judge. That is something that is reserved for God alone.

I believe that the reason many of our non-charismatic brethren will not come and set a foot in the PTL Club is because they are afraid to be associated with charismatics. But, praise God, He's been breaking that wall down. I'm meeting privately with many of them. They still won't come on the air, but I'm meeting in fellowship with them. That is a great step, for a few years ago they wouldn't even walk down the street with me. And recently many of those who did not adhere to the charismatic movement have been coming on PTL one by one to talk about their books and their records. And it thrills my heart to be able to share with them the air time that God has made available to us through the PTL Club. For I love them, even though our personal doctrine might not agree.

One of the greatest obstacles that I had to overcome while I was hosting the 700 Club on the early days of television was the audience reaction to the guests I interviewed. I would receive letters or phone calls or someone would come to me and say, "Did you know that you had so-and-so on your program, and he has done this, or he has done that, or he doesn't believe this or that doctrine, or he's Armenian or Calvinist, or etc.

I became so upset inwardly that I finally got an ulcer. I was sick trying to figure out who was right and who was wrong, who was of God and who wasn't of God.

Finally one day I was driving home and was stopped for a red light. And at that time the teaching on praising God for everything was at its peak. So I sat there at the stop light praising God for the red light. To this day I still don't know why. And I believed it was rather foolish, but that was what the teaching was, so, I, like everybody else, was just sitting there praising God for a red light. And as I was waiting, the Lord spoke quietly to me, and asked, "Jim Bakker, who do you think you are? Do you think you're God?"

Of course my quick reply was, "God, of course I don't think I'm You. I'm not that foolish."

Then He quietly said, "Then why are you trying to do My job? You're not Me. You're not big enough to be Me. And don't you ever forget it. Jim Bakker, that's why you're sick. You're a servant, not a god. Your responsibility is to love Me and to love those that love

Me. You're trying to do my work. You're trying to be a judge, and that is not your concern."

"But God," I replied, "what am I going to do? All these charismatics and other people keep telling me I have so-and-so on, and, Jesus, I've tried my best. I don't want to offend anybody."

And again I heard God speak. And He said, "Jim, I'll make a deal with you. (And making a deal with God is a pretty good deal. He really said that. I remember it as clearly as if it were a second ago.) Jim Bakker, you love them, and I will judge them."

"What a deal," I thought. And instantly I felt the glory of the Lord come upon me and His peace enter into my very being. It was like the load of the world came toppling off my shoulders. Tears came running down my cheeks as I realized that all God was asking me to do was to love them. And He would judge them. Oh, what a lesson I learned. For, you see, that day my life was turned around. After all, what God had spoken to me was certainly Scripture. For the Word tells us in Matthew 7:1, "Judge not, that ye be not judged."

Do we really believe the Word? It says, "Judge not." And yet we don't forgive our friends, our neighbors, our husbands, our wives. In essence we become a mad bomber. Yes, a mad bomber—because we are blowing up the bridge of redemption. And that also is scriptural, for the Scripture tells us that when we don't forgive, we destroy the bridge of forgiveness to the cross. And because we don't forgive, we won't be forgiven.

I believe that is one of the greatest reasons today why we have a sick church and sick people in the church. That's why there are miserable charismatics and miserable non-charismatics—because we are judging everybody when we have no right to judge. We have destroyed our own forgiveness. Now, friend, that's the Bible. Those aren't my words. They're the words of God Himself. We must love, love, love. For love covers a multitude of sin.

Oral Roberts (in insert) stands in front of his vision for the City of Faith as he first presents it to his television audience. In September of 1980 Oral again speaks to his television audience—this time with the City of Faith over half completed and towering in the Tulsa, Oklahoma, sky.

People worship in the newly completed Crystal Cathedral in Garden Grove, California, where Robert Schuller is pastor.

Rex Humbard and his family minister to thousands in a packed stadium in Brazil.

4

Renewing the Mind

Romans 12 is one of the most thought provoking chapters in the Scripture. It begins in verse one with the words, "I beseech you therefore, brethren, by the mercies of God, that ye present your bodies a living sacrifice, holy, acceptable unto God, which is your reasonable service." We are being told by God to present our bodies as a living sacrifice. It is just the reasonable thing to do—there's nothing terrific or great. It's just something that's expected of all Christians— that we should be holy and that we should be acceptable unto God.

We're told in the second verse that we should not be conformed to the world, but "be ye transformed by the renewing of your mind." We no longer can hate because we're hated or love because we're loved or give because it's been given unto us. Instead, we must act in accordance with the will of God and the Scripture and love those who do not love us, give to those who do not give to us, and return love for hatred. This is the will of God!

Romans twelve continues through verse eight to mention which gifts operate within the Body of Christ. We are also instructed that we have many members, but we are one body. We are the Body of Jesus Christ.

Verse nine helps us begin to see the work of a transformed life in Jesus Christ. We're told to "let love be without dissimulation" or hypocrisy. And that means that we should hate the very presence of sin and should not touch it, but, instead, we should embrace good things.

In verse ten we read that we should "be kindly affectioned one to another with brotherly love; in honour preferring one another." I suppose this is very hard for us to do, because it means letting others be first, letting others receive honor, letting others receive the glory. It means being kind and courteous and thoughtful.

Verse eleven tells us to be "not slothful in business; fervent in spirit; serving the Lord." God wants us as Christians to bring honor to Him in all that we do. In our daily walk and in our work we as God's children should be the very best in the world—if a carpenter, the very best carpenter in the world; if a baker, the best baker in the world; if a preacher, the most anointed preacher; if a tentmaker, we should make the best tents known to man.

Verse twelve tells us to be "rejoicing in hope; patient in tribulation, continuing instant in prayer." In all things we should be concerned that our attitude should always stress the Christ-like spirit of Jesus coming from us.

Verse thirteen directs us to distribute "to the necessity of saints" and be "given to hospitality." We should be sure that we share that which we have with our brothers and sisters in Jesus.

The Scripture continues in verses fourteen and fifteen, "Bless them which persecute you: bless, and curse not. Rejoice with them that do rejoice, and weep with them that weep." Oh, how hard it is to take these verses to heart, because the first thing that most of us want to do is to retaliate, get back, and to put the other brother lower than we, and not to overcome the persecution with our simple love. We should rejoice to see others happy, and yet we should have sympathy when they're in grief. But above all, we should strive to be one in Jesus.

Verse sixteen to the end of the chapter gives us many charges that we should keep. "Be of the same mind one toward another. Mind not high things, but condescend to men of low estate. Be not wise in your own conceits. Recompense to no man evil for evil. Provide things honest in the sight of all men. If it be possible, as much as lieth in you, live peaceably with all men.

"Dearly beloved, avenge not yourselves, but rather give place unto wrath: for it is written, Vengeance is mine; I will repay, saith the Lord. Therefore if thine enemy hunger, feed him; if he thirst, give him drink: for in so doing thou shalt heap coals of fire on his head. Be not overcome of evil, but overcome evil with good." All of this simply means that we must not always strive to be with the high and mighty, but be willing to even associate with Jesus' nobodies.

Today, personal success and financial gain seem to be supreme in many lives. I recently read a book where a man said, "Don't associate with anyone that cannot lift your financial standard or your personal goal. Only have friends that are successful." But, I'm afraid that those words were not spoken by the Spirit of Christ or from the Word of God.

"Be not wise in your own conceits" is one of the harder directions to follow, because we tend to think that we know everything, and we often prove that we do not have a teachable spirit.

How important it is that we do not take things into our own hands and try to repay evil for evil, for God is the One who can handle our enemy.

We should also be aware of how what we're doing looks to others and strive that they might see the Christ-walk in us.

It is so easy today to break the peace within the Body, to sow that discord. The Scripture here tells us that we should be peacemakers and not peacebreakers—that we should not have contention in our home or in the church or where we work or within the Body.

We should never try to justify what we do or defend God. We should simply be quiet and speak not a word.

Yes, it's time that we begin loving those who hate us so that we can melt that opposition by using the burning fire of the love of Jesus Christ.

There are many hindrances that keep us from being what God would have us be. If we value that special walk with Jesus, there are things that we should try to avoid that are very dangerous.

Living in any known sin is perhaps the greatest bottleneck to our walk. These beams in our eyes (Matt. 7:3) will not let us see Jesus as we should. There will be a wall between us and God. Even when we try to study the Word, our sin will look us in the face and say, "These things do not belong to you." When we take so much pleasure in sin, we can't come to Jesus in peace. Every intentional sin will be to our happiness as water is to fire. It will quench our joy. It will disable us so that we can no more serve Jesus than a bird can fly with clipped wings. We certainly need to pray daily: "Jesus, 'lead us not into temptation, but deliver us from evil' " (Matt. 6:13).

When our minds are on things below (glorying in our carnal prosperity), and not on Christ, we are simply rejoicing in hope of earthly success—not Jesus.

We must keep earthly possessions as loose as a light jacket so that we may take them off at will. We must let Jesus be close to our hearts, remembering constantly that friendship with the world puts us at odds with God. James 4:4 says, "The friendship of the world is enmity with God."

"Love not the world, neither the things that are in the world. If any man love the world, the love of the Father is not in him" (1 John 2:15). That's pretty plain. If you want to be really happy, absorb that verse into your heart.

Of course, we cannot avoid the ungodly in business dealings or from helping them, and certainly not if we're ever going to draw them to a saving knowledge of the Lord Jesus. However, we should not let worldly fellowship have a chance to draw us away from Jesus. We should be very careful that they do not harm our fellowship with the Lord. We should also be very careful of having fellowship with people whose conversation is empty and who will divert our thoughts from Jesus. We need all the help we can get for our Christian walk here on earth.

Today, TV can be our greatest blessing or our greatest curse. Most of the TV is filling our minds with profanity, filthiness, violence and crime, and attitudes that we would not normally admire in our friends. Rarely does secular television lift our thoughts to Jesus. We shouldn't be surprised that Satan would have us watch more television than he would have us be in the Word of God.

Satan always tries to make us think only of ourselves and our own pleasure. He often uses TV to let us live in a selfish fantasy world and to put ourselves first. A person whose faith is centered in himself and his own opinions will be most frequently and enthusiastically mouthing it, but he whose faith lies in the knowledge and love of God and in the depth of His Word will be most delightfully speaking and living it.

The least controversial doctrines are usually the most important and most necessary to know. "Foolish and unlearned questions avoid, knowing that they do gender strifes. And the servant of the Lord must not strive" (2 Tim. 2:23-24). "But avoid foolish questions, and genealogies, and contentions, and strivings about the law; for they are unprofitable and vain" (Titus 3:9).

It's absolutely amazing what happens when we come into real Biblical truths. For example, let's look at the baptism of the Holy Spirit. Some people become so proud and high and mighty, thinking that they have something that no one else has. At that point I believe they lose most of what they had. So we must be careful of that proud and high and mighty spirit. For it was that spirit that got the angels chased out of Heaven.

Most of the time when we've had a soul humbling day or a time of trouble or when we're the lowest, that's the time we have the freest access to God. James 4:6 tells us, "God resisteth the proud, but giveth grace unto the humble." When we are the driest, we catch fire the easiest.

Are you glad when you hear of your popularity and depressed when you hear that others criticize you? Do you love those best that honor you? Are you angry when your will is crossed? Can you serve God in a low place as well as in a high place? Are you more ready to defend yourself than confess your faults? Can you scarcely take criticism? Well, if these symptoms are in our lives, we might as well chalk it up that we're proud. That isn't the Spirit of Christ moving, but the spirit of Satan. A proud man makes himself his god and sets himself up as his own idol. This is such a common and dangerous sin, and yet we hardly recognize it.

Many today want to get to Heaven by just sitting. And yet we're reminded again and again that we're soldiers of the cross, that we are laborers together with Christ. James so readily says, "Show me your works, and I'll show you your faith," and "Faith without works is dead." Yet, it is so easy to be ruled by a lazy spirit. We want to lie down at the foot of the hill and look to the top, wishing we were there without the climb. And you and I know that will not happen.

How many people read books and hear sermon after sermon, expecting to hear of an easy walk and easy way. They ask for directions for the Christ-life as if hearing would be sufficient. But if we show them their works and tell them they cannot have these delights on easier terms, then they leave us, as the young man left Christ—sorrowful (Matt. 19:22).

It was the custom of ancient Parthians not to give their children any breakfast until they saw the sweat on their faces from some type of work. I believe we will find this to be God's usual way—not to give His children a taste of His delicacies until they begin to perspire by seeking and serving Him.

We live in an age where everybody wants instant this and instant that. We want instant holiness without being holy. We want instant rewards without doing anything to deserve them. And God wants us to prepare for battle.

God is calling us to battle. He wants us to begin waging the war. He doesn't want us only to prepare, but He wants us out there fighting the fight of faith. He wants us instant in season and out of season to speak for Him.

While visiting in Arkansas, I attended the *Great Passion Play* in Eureka Springs. How vividly this portrayal makes the Scripture come to life. As the actors spoke the words of Jesus, how they seemed to pierce my heart. I have heard almost from childhood the words, "I want you to love one another; I want you to love your neighbor as yourself," but when I heard them spoken in the play, the reality of those words came over me, and I realized how little I really have loved my neighbor.

Love covers a multitude of sins. First Corinthians 13, which is the "love chapter," has been read time and time and time again from the pulpit, but it seems so few Christians understand the depth of its meaning. We are told there that if we "speak with the tongues of men and of angels and have not love," we are as sounding brass and tinkling cymbals. Yet how much emphasis some charismatics today put on tongues and how little on loving.

"And though I have the gift of prophecy, and understand all mysteries, and all knowledge; and though I have all faith, so that I could remove mountains, and have not love, I am nothing." Look what that does to the gifts that we move in and even to the message of faith that we hear so much today. It is all nothing without love.

I myself speak a lot on tithing, and believe in it, and

yet the Scripture here tells us in verse three, "And though I bestow all my goods to feed the poor, and though I give my body to be burned, and have not love, it profiteth me nothing," or does me no good whatsoever. I believe that so few of us as God's children know the first bit about what real love is. It doesn't envy, it suffers long, it is never puffed up, it doesn't seek its own way, it always behaves right, it doesn't get provoked, it doesn't think evil of one another, it doesn't rejoice in sin or iniquity. Just stop and think of those that I've listed so far from the Scripture—how if we really practiced this, there would be no talebearing, there would be no backbiting, there would be no jealousy or strife or contention or animosity. We would stop condemning others in the Body of Christ. Instead, we would be lifting up Jesus continually.

How we seem to rejoice today when a brother stumbles, but according to this, if we really had the love of Jesus abiding in us, we would weep and be mournful when a brother stumbled. We would strive to gently pick him up and restore that fellowship.

Love really would rejoice in truth. It bears all things, it believes all things, it hopes all things, and endures all things.

Oh, my friend, how we need to meditate day and night on this chapter in 1 Corinthians and let the Spirit of God burn it into the very depths of our spirits, that we could begin walking in the truth of the Word of God.

Love never fails. Everything else will fail, but love will not. For, you see, it really boils down to the fact that God is love. And if we're going to have a Christ-like disposition, then we must put on love.

I had a very close friend whose marriage was in trouble. And I knew that if God did not intervene, a divorce would soon be following. One afternoon the Lord spoke to me and said, "Jim, you love that marriage like you love your own marriage. Don't you let them divorce."

And I said, "What? What do you mean that I shouldn't let them divorce?"

And the Lord said, "Dedicate yourself to that couple. Love them and save that marriage whatever the cost."

And I thought to myself, "Do I love them that much? Do I love them enough to get up in the middle of the night and fly to them or pray for them or counsel with them to save their marriage?"

And the Lord spoke to me through His Word. He said, "If you want to love Me, you love your neighbor as yourself." And Mark 12:33 came to mind. It states, "And to love him with all the heart, and with all the understanding, and with all the soul, and with all the strength, and to love his neighbour as himself, is more than all whole burnt offerings and sacrifices."

Isn't it amazing how simple the Word of God is and how complex we make it simply because we have a fear of loving. We must love each other. We must begin preferring and honoring one another. The Word tells us that the world will know that we are His because we have love one for another.

The Full Gospel Businessmen's motto is "His banner over us is love." That, my friend, is the ingredient that the world is looking for—it is love. It is love that is seen in the unity of the Body of Christ—not in the hate and dissension and strife; not in discord and violence and fragmented segments that the world sees today.

5

The Acts
of Love

Jesus in His great prayer in the seventeenth
chapter of John prayed that we would be one as He and
the Father are one. I believe that when we are one, ONE,
the world will be won, WON. I believe with my entire
being that the greatest hindrance to world evangelism is
the lack of love and unity in the Body of Jesus Christ.

How sad it is—how very sad—that we who know
Jesus are so divided.

I've had so many people come to me and say, "Jim,
you preachers all preach, but you don't work together.
There are no organizations working together, no
churches working together. There is such division. All of
you strive to build your own little empires. Why?"

Sometimes that's very hard to answer, but I believe
the era of "I'd rather do it myself" is over. We will either
have each other and love each other or, I believe, we will
have nothing. No man can be an island unto himself, for

we must realize that there is only one Body and one Spirit, one Lord, one baptism, and one Bridegroom—the person of Jesus Christ.

I believe the attacks we have seen in recent months on the Church and on Christian television most likely have been in the plan and the will of God, because at last it will bring the Body of Jesus Christ together. So we should rejoice in adversity.

Several months ago Oral Roberts came to PTL. Do you know what he did? He raised money for me, for my ministry, on national television. He kicked off my telethon, not for the City of Faith, but for PTL. Now that's preferring one another. That's helping one another. That's love in action. That's faith backed by love.

Maybe I'm the new kid on the block. There are many who have been on the block longer than I have. But what a joy it is that they now have reached out their hands to help me. Rex Humbard has given us all the use of their computer technology to help solve our computer problems at PTL. My general manager not long ago spent the entire day with Pat Robertson, discussing how the two networks could better serve each other. Paul Crouch has been talking with us about how we could better serve by unity in various projects for the kingdom of God.

Not long ago Oral Roberts and PTL came to an agreement. Oral Roberts built a great earth station on the campus of Oral Roberts University, and Oral Roberts is now coming live into the homes of America on the PTL Television Network—two ministries working together to bring back the King of Kings and the Lord of Lords. Because we are in the kingdom of God, we must build only one kingdom.

Again I want to emphasize that if Oral Roberts is shot down, Jim Bakker is going to suffer. If 700 goes under, we all go under. If Paul Crouch, Billy Graham, Jerry Falwell, or anyone else goes under, we're all in danger. We must stand together in unity in the Body of Jesus Christ so we can win the world to Jesus. I know that in the end we win. Yes. We win, we win, we win! And those who turn their backs on God are the losers.

Christ prayed in John 17:21-23:

That they all may be one; as thou, Father, art in me, and I in thee, that they also may be one in us: that the world may believe that thou hast sent me. And the glory which thou gavest me, I have given them; that they may be one, even as we are one: I in them, and thou in me, that they may be made perfect in one; and that the world may know that thou hast sent me, and hast loved them, as thou hast loved me.

As a young man, I had the privilege of sitting at the feet of a wonderful pastor and his wife. Sister Olson would teach me all about the love of God. As she taught me, she would make Jesus so real that tears would stream down my face. Then I would pray, "Oh, God, my prayer is that someday I can make the love of God real to people." Today, I believe the world is still hungry for that kind of love.

Sister Olson also began to share a message about Jesus, where she called Him "God's beachcomber." The beachcomber walks the shores of the beach and picks up bits of wrecked ships and pieces of wood in which nobody else can see any beauty. But the beachcomber picks up those old pieces of wrecked ships and makes something beautiful out of them.

"Jesus was God's beachcomber," she continued, "walking the shores of this old world, picking up wrecked lives and putting the pieces back together again, loving the unlovely, loving those whom nobody else cares about."

I want you to know that Jesus, right now, is walking all around this land with outstretched arms saying, "Come unto me all ye that labor and are heavy laden." I believe in this hour it is the job of the Church of Jesus Christ to love now, to reach out now to a sick and dying world! Second Corinthians 6:2 says, "Behold, now is the accepted time; behold, now is the day of salvation."

A message that God is speaking loud and clear to the Church today is that we must love one another; that the charismatics love the non-charismatics; that the black love the white and the white love the black; that we reach out to love the unlovely; and that we love those of different denominations.

When movie stars get together, they all give each other awards. Recently, I watched a roast on television and I got to thinking, "How could we Christian leaders all get together and honor any one member?" It would be difficult just to get a group of people together; and then, who would we honor? I thought of one man who had been in the ministry for a long time, and so I felt he would be good. Then I thought, "Who would come?"

You know, the movie stars all give awards to one another, and they seem to love each other. How much more should the Church of Jesus Christ begin to get together! Politicians get together, and they don't even trust each other. Fraternities—they all get together. One time I stopped at a hotel where a group of young doctors, who had gone to college together, were gathered having a good time. They hadn't forgotten each other.

Beloved, if God so loved us, we ought also to love one another. Your Christian love will change lives. Your Christian love will transform others.

When I was living in California, a family began to watch the PTL Club. That family had not been out of their home much for several years because they were overweight and embarrassed to go out in public. They began to watch the PTL Club, and somehow the love of God came through the program into their living room. They began to call us and write us. Tammy and I began to take them out for drives. This was the first time in several years they had come out of their own home. They were afraid people would laugh at them. Love began to change their lives.

Ecclesiastes 11:1 tells us that bread cast upon the waters shall return after many days. Well, there soon was a time when we were in desperate need. I had nowhere to turn and no income. It was the lady and her son who fed Tammy, me, our family, and our staff. They brought food to our home every few days and packed our freezer. When you reach out in love, don't expect anything in return. But you are going to get something in return because what you sow, you will reap.

A while back I invited a Jewish man to come be my guest on PTL. He wanted to talk about the Holocaust which interests me much, for I love the Jewish people. Mr. Goldberg came and shared. We prayed together, and I prayed that the God of Abraham, Isaac, and Jacob would bring us together and unite us in God. A few weeks later, Mr. Goldberg said, "I can't understand it. You haven't tried to convert me yet. I have become a good friend of yours, and I don't pass my friendship out to just anyone, but you all have something."

I want to share with you the conclusion of this story. We have a local radio station that makes fun of Christianity and PTL, and I want you to know that about the only person in Charlotte, North Carolina, who publicly came out and spoke in behalf of PTL was Mr. Goldberg, my Jewish friend. God says, "You love them; I'll judge them." Luke 6:37 reads, "Judge not, and ye shall not be judged: condemn not, and you shall not be condemned: forgive, and ye shall be forgiven."

If the Church of Jesus Christ and the members that profess to be a part of the Body of Christ will stop judging one another and begin to love, we are going to turn the world upside down.

Many people have felt that spirituality is pious praying, pious demonstration, and pious worship. Jesus had much to say about that kind of participation without love. Dr. Palmer (a great theologian) recently said on our broadcast, that after long research he has come to the conclusion that spirituality is not worship to God, but how you treat your fellow man, how you treat those around you.

How important this is! First John 4:20 states: "If a man say, I love God, and hateth his brother, he is a liar; for he that loveth not his brother whom he hath seen, how can he love God whom he hath not seen."

If you want to love God, love your fellow man. Love that Catholic priest, love that protestant pastor, that nun, that sister, that worker in the other denomination. Love one another and demonstrate the love of God; because if you can't love them, how can you love a God whom you cannot see? Serving God is more than lip service.

If I was with a brother and said, "I love you, I love you, I love you, I love you," he would like that for a while, but soon he would say, "Why don't you do something if you really love me?"

If I really loved him, I would demonstrate that love. I would take care of his children if they were sick. He could then say, "Jim Bakker really loves me." If his wife needed help and I helped his wife, he would say, "Oh, that is a wonderful thing. He is helping my wife." In helping his family I would be demonstrating my love. It is the same way with God. If you love God, then love His family—because that is next to the heart of God. Jesus Himself declared that our demonstration of love to others was equal to doing the same for Him: "Verily I say unto you, Inasmuch as ye have done it unto one of the least of these my brethren, ye have done it unto me" (Matt. 25:40).

Love's actions speak louder than words in any relationship. Suppose Tammy and I, for example, walked together and talked together and did everything together. We just loved each other so much. Everything we did, we asked each other about it. And then I got in the middle of a large crowd, and all of a sudden I dropped down on my knees and loudly said, "Oh, Tammy, you are so wonderful!" What would she think?

People say, "I fellowship with God," but they only show off when they get in a prayer meeting, or they only demonstrate their love to God when they get in a crowd. Hey, where is their walk with God? Serving God is more than lip service. It is a relationship. If you have faith and you wonder why you don't get answers to prayers, let me read the answer from Galatians 5:6, "For in Jesus Christ neither circumcision availeth any thing, nor uncircumcision; but faith which worketh by love." Your faith goes into action through love.

I think of Mark Buntain, the great missionary to India, and all of the thousands of little children he has helped feed. He loves to help people in any way he can. One day he was driving down the street and saw a man waiting for a cab in the rain. So Mark Buntain stopped to pick up this man, and the man said, "No, I'll catch a cab."

But Mark said, "No, I want to take you where you are going." He had compassion for the man standing in the rain.

A year or two after that, Mark was trying to build a hospital in Calcutta, India. He had one more permit to obtain and was having a rough time getting approval to build the hospital. He walked into the room of the government official who could grant the last permit, and guess who was sitting behind the desk? The man in the rain! God honors you when you reach out to touch others.

Loving each other is a proof to us that we are born-again. "We know that we have passed from death unto life, because we love the brethren. He that loveth not his brother abideth in death" (1 John 3:14).

This is God's Word. It is how you know you are saved, born-again into the Body of Christ. If you are born-again, Galatians 5:22-26 is for you. This is the fruit of a born-again Christian:

But the fruit of the Spirit is love, joy, peace, longsuffering, gentleness, goodness, faith, meekness, temperance: against such there is no law. And they that are Christ's have crucified the flesh with the affections and lusts. If we live in the Spirit, let us also walk in the Spirit. Let us not be desirous of vain glory, provoking one another, envying one another.

This is the spirit of the born-again Christian. What is the spirit of those who will not inherit eternal life, the lost? Galatians 5:19-21 taken from the Living Bible says:

But when you follow your own wrong inclinations, your lives will produce these evil results: impure thoughts, eagerness for lustful pleasure, idolatry, spiritism (that is encouraging the activities of demons), hatred and fighting, jealousy and anger, constant effort to get the best for yourself, complaints and criticisms, the feeling that everyone else is wrong except those in your own little group—and there will be wrong doctrine, envy, murder, drunkenness, wild parties, and all sorts of things. Let me tell you again as I have before, that anyone living that sort of life will not inherit the kingdom of God.

This is the fruit of the flesh, and those who do such things will not inherit the kingdom of God. I trust this day if your life is not filled with the fruit of the Spirit, but the fruits of death and the flesh, that you will ask God to let you draw close to Him and become a part of the family of God. One of the problems we face today in the Church is not the world outside but the world inside—the organized church, the body or local assembly. It is so important that we, who name the name of Jesus Christ are not guilty of dividing the Body of Christ.

Recently I read an article from a newspaper in

Charlottesville, Virginia. The headline read "Prayer Guides Campaign of a Born-Again Candidate." I've known this great gentleman for years; he is a car dealer in Norfolk, Virginia. He is a wonderful man and stated in this article that God had called him to run for a political office.

The only group making a negative statement came from one of the largest known religious bodies in the world. They came out against him and told people to beware of anybody who professes to be a born-again Christian in politics.

We see this happening time and again. Laws passed that hinder the church have been instigated because one member wanted to get back at some other religious body. But these people will someday fall into the very trap they have set for their brothers. It is so important that we reach out. We cannot control what any religious body or what any other person does, but we can control what *we* do.

What would happen if we would love those who are unlovely and those who are into drugs, and all the other things that we preach against?

If we would love them and win them to Jesus, we would clean up the pornography, the sin, and the lust right at its very root. It is so important that the Church love the unlovely, that we love those whom we do not understand, that we love those we disagree with and we show them the love of God. Loving does not mean we condone the sin, but simply means we love the sinner.

My brother died when he was only 40 years old. As he lay dying, I began to remember something in his life. It was the last time he ever went into a church. In that church my father was head usher. For some reason my brother had rebelled against God, but that night my father and mother brought him back to church, and for the first time he was back in a service.

During the service the offering was to be taken, and my father asked my brother to take up the offering with him since no one else was sitting in the back. Whether he was right or wrong, he felt it would be a good thing. But the wife of the pastor of the church came up quickly and took the offering plate from my brother's hands and said, "You are not fit to receive the offering." My brother never walked into another church the rest of his life.

I flew to see him a few years ago as he lay dying in the Veteran's Hospital of a rare disease. For the first time in my life, I was able to tell my brother I loved him. We had been separated so long by so much.

As he lay dying, he wanted to see my cousin, Margie, the only person he knew that loved him. In his dying moments, he climbed on an airplane and flew to Pasadena. Like a dying animal in the last moment of life trying to find love, he went to her home. As she loved hime and prayed with him, he accepted Jesus Christ as his personal Savior. I had prayed for Bob all his life, and at every service I would raise my hand and say, "Pray for my brother Bob." But there in his moment of death, he dragged his weakened body to the only person he knew that really loved him.

At his death he requested that there be no funeral, and I know why—because he didn't think anyone would come. He died alone.

Oh, people, let's love and leave the judging to God!

6
Key Words
for Survival

There can be no thought of survival without applying the following three words to our vocabulary and life: trust, delight, commit.

Trust is used in the Old Testament and *believe* is its counterpart in the New Testament.

I've found that when I really trust God, I have confidence in Him that He will not fail me. I can absolutely rely on Him and His Word and know that God isn't going to pull the rug out from under me.

I know the fear that runs through people's hearts. Sometimes we think that if we dedicate our child to God, the Lord will take that child. I've known young people who feared giving their lives to Christ because they erroneously thought God would send them off as missionaries to the darkest reaches of Africa. Tammy Faye had that problem in her teen years.

One of the great fears that faces us today is that God

really will not care for us. We must learn to trust God completely. And the more we know God, the more we can trust Him.

God is not trying to spoil your life. He loves you. He is simply trying to bring each of us to a point of surrender to His master plan for our lives. Job had obviously found that place. In spite of all the trouble and woe that fell upon him, Job was able to say, "Though he slay me, yet will I trust in him" (Job 13:15).

Many recall the rich young ruler who came to Jesus seeking to follow Him. Knowing where the young ruler's true interest lay, Jesus said, "Give up all that you have and follow me."

The Word then states what the response was: "And he was sad at that saying, and went away grieved: for he had great possessions" (Mark 10:22).

Some think if the rich young ruler had done what Jesus said, he would have been forced to live in poverty. A few actually teach poverty as a way of life. I don't know any place in the Bible where it states poverty is spiritual. All Jesus was trying to get from the rich young ruler was total commitment.

In that same passage of Scripture Jesus declares, "There is no man that hath left house, or brethren, or sisters, or father, or mother, or wife, or children, or lands, for my sake, and the gospel's, but he shall receive a hundredfold now in this time, . . . and in the world to come eternal life" (Mark 10:29-30).

Anytime I see people giving to God, He is always multiplying it back to them.

The Apostle Paul boldly declares in Philippians 4:19, "But my God shall supply all your need according to his riches in glory by Christ Jesus." How will God provide? The Apostle says the measure will be "according to his riches in glory."

That leads to the inevitable question, "How rich is God in glory?" Revelation 21:18-21 gives the following description of the New Jerusalem where the Lord resides:

> And the building of the wall of it was of jasper: and the city was pure gold, like unto clear glass.
>
> And the foundations of the wall of the city were garnished with all manner of precious stones. The first foundation was jasper; the second, sapphire; the third, a chalcedony; the fourth, an emerald; the fifth, sardonyx; the sixth, sardius; the seventh, chrysolite; the eighth, beryl; the ninth, a topaz; the tenth, a chrysoprasus; the eleventh, a jacinth; the twelfth, an amethyst.
>
> And the twelve gates were twelve pearls; every several gate was of one pearl: and the street of the city was pure gold, as it were transparent glass.

Your Heavenly Father is rich. He is not poor. Look at these Scriptures which detail the Lord's possessions:

". . . For all the earth is mine" (Exod. 19:5).

"For every beast of the forest is mine, and the cattle upon a thousand hills" (Ps. 50:10).

"The silver is mine, and the gold is mine, saith the Lord of hosts" (Hag. 2:8).

I believe that if the rich young ruler had simply trusted Jesus, the situation would have been much different. If he had said, "Lord, I'm willing to give it all up. It's all yours," I believe the Lord would have given it all back, plus a hundred times more.

God wants us to know He has the answer to our problems. He knows our needs and is vitally concerned with our situation.

Who better than God would know how to handle our problems? After all, if the Creator of heaven and earth has gone to the trouble of sending His only Son into the world to redeem you, doesn't it make sense He's equally concerned with your other problems?

"Are not five sparrows sold for two farthings, and not one of them is forgotten before God? But even the very hairs of your head are all numbered. Fear not therefore: ye are of more value than many sparrows" (Luke 12:6-7).

We can rely on God's Word. He cannot fail. He has never failed. Listen to the words of the psalmist, who had discovered this marvelous truth about God. "As for God, his way is perfect: the word of the Lord is tried: he is a buckler to all those that trust in him" (Ps. 18:30).

God has the best in store for you. God has not called us to do something unattainable. If I can run PTL with all my fears, insecurities, and doubts, you can do what God wants you to do, too.

"Be delighted with the Lord. Then he will give you all your heart's desires" (Ps. 37:4 LB).

When we begin to delight in the Lord, it becomes natural to praise Him. "The joy of the Lord is your strength" (Neh. 8:10). By delighting in Him, we can keep spiritually strong.

Most of us start out delighting in God, but then we're hit with a problem and our disposition turns sour. But that's when we should be joyful and delight in God!

The prophet Habakkuk records just such a terrible situation. "The fig tree shall not blossom, neither shall fruit be in the vines; the labor of the olive shall fail; and the fields shall yield no meat; the flock shall be cut off from the fold, and there shall be no herd in the stalls" (Hab. 3:17). Yet, in the face of this, Habakkuk declares in verse 18, "Yet I will rejoice in the Lord, I will joy in the God of my salvation."

We can do the same things in our lives. When things go wrong, we claim Romans 8:28 and delight in adversity. "And we know that all things work together for good to them that love God, to them who are the called according to his purpose."

All things work together for good—not just part but all. That includes the problems we're facing right now. That includes the situation that's hounding our lives. Because we have learned to trust God, we can praise Him for all things working in our lives.

Praising God in all situations is not easy. It goes against all of man's intellect. It simply doesn't make sense. But none of God's ways makes sense to the natural man.

I grew up in a church from a major pentecostal denomination—a demonination that prides itself on proclaiming the full gospel. Yet, very few of us knew how to praise God outside of the church service. Many times I wanted to praise God, but I felt like my jaws were wired shut and the praise was bottled up within me.

Praising or delighting in God is simply an act of the will. I can either choose to praise God, or I can sit around with the problem on my shoulders and choose not to.

What happens to people who don't learn to praise God? Deuteronomy 28:47-48 in the Living Bible gives a sober warning. "You will become slaves to your enemies because of your failure to praise God for all that he has given you. The Lord will send your enemies against you, and you will be hungry, thirsty, naked, and in want for everything. A yoke of iron shall be placed around your neck until you are destroyed!"

What happens to people who are always grumbling and complaining? If they're sick, they stay sick. Why? Because they have failed to praise God. They have actually become slaves to their enemies—sickness, poverty, death, and all the rest.

Jesus has redeemed us from the curse of sin, sickness, and poverty. How can evil dwell within us if we are praising God? It can't. Praise will drive off the enemies of your soul. It is a weapon given to Christians by our Heavenly Father.

It's the same when somebody talks wrongly about you. Defending yourself, you decide to fight back by slandering them. In the process you have become a slave to them. Jesus said, "All they that take the sword shall perish with the sword" (Matt. 26:52).

Before his calamity, Job was a wealthy man. But during his time of trouble, Job did not sin with his lips (Job 2:10). And as a result "the Lord blessed the latter end of Job more than his beginning" (Job 42:12). In short, the Lord doubled everything Job had before. That's a measure of God's great love and blessing to His children, even today!

God wants us to delight ourselves in Him. When we begin delighting in God, we are saying, "God, whatever you want, I want. I give you total charge of my life." As we confess that statement to God, a new joy will flow into our lives. Along with that joy will come a sense of power and strength. It will push us into a new dimension of mastery over the problems of life.

"Commit thy way unto the Lord; trust also in him; and he shall bring it to pass" (Ps. 37:5). God wants us to commit our way to Him. In this case, the word *way* means *everything*!

When we give our money or jewelry to a bank for safekeeping, they put it in a safety deposit box and lock it up in a big vault. The bank is holding these items in trust for us. That's exactly what God wants us to do with our problems. He wants us to deposit them with Him.

God wants us to entrust Him with each and every situation we face. If we trust in this way, He gives us the promise, "He shall bring it to pass." That's our dividend from the Lord. He will solve the problem. He will keep us safe.

Winning by giving up is contrary to man's plans, but it works with God.

In 1972 when I left an important position with the Christian Broadcasting Network, I had no idea the Lord had plans to create the PTL Television Network. When I left CBN, I was simply following the direction of the Holy Spirit.

The night of our farewell at CBN, I walked out of the building wondering, "What am I going to do now?" The future was unknown. All I knew was that I was following God.

In time, following God meant conducting telethons around the country and temporarily hosting another Christian talk-variety program in Los Angeles. But ultimately, Tammy and I came to Charlotte, and the PTL Club was born. Today, the PTL Television Network is the largest purchaser of television air time outside the three major networks—ABC, NBC, and CBS.

Would PTL have become a reality without such a commitment on my part? I seriously doubt it.

Proverbs 3:5-6 gives a picture of the committed life. "Trust in the Lord with all thine heart; and lean not unto thine own understanding. In all thy ways acknowledge him, and he shall direct thy paths."

In my case, I didn't know the path was leading to Charlotte and the founding of the PTL Television Network. All I did was commit myself to the Lord and follow Him as doors opened or closed. In doing that, God's will was accomplished.

The Hebrew word for "commit" is *galal*. It means "to roll on" or "wallow in." When we commit a problem to God, then we can roll or wallow in His goodness. We've abandoned ourselves to Him. The whole problem now belongs to God.

This sense of giving up or abandoning ourselves to God works in many practical ways. When Tammy and I first came to Charlotte, we had planned to be here for only a few days. But during the telethon I was conducting, God moved in a miraculous way. People were saved by the hundreds, cancers dropped off bodies, and tumors vanished.

Just like a voice in the night, the Holy Spirit said, "Jim, what more do I have to tell you to do than to make your home base in Charlotte?"

"No more, Lord," I answered. "You don't have to say anything else. I believe you. Your anointing is here, and I want to be where your anointing is."

Immediately I flew back to California to sell our house. I was a little concerned about the house because Tammy had hung pictures everywhere. Not just a few pictures either—she had hung picture galleries. You walked into the house, and an entire wall was covered with pictures. Since houses show much better with the furniture in place, I was praying for a quick sale.

Two months later when the sale was supposed to close, I got a telephone call. It was a real estate man in California. "Reverend Bakker," he said unhappily, "the deal on your house fell through."

It was a bombshell. The news hit me like a wet towel smack in the face. "Oh, Lord," I moaned, thinking about the empty house and the walls full of holes as if some wild machine gunner had raked it. "I'll never make it now," I said dejectedly.

Right at that instant I wanted to wallow in self-pity.

Fortunately Tammy was standing nearby. "Wait a minute," she said sharply. "You've been preaching that once we've committed a problem to God, we ought not to take it again. Jim, you've got to practice what you preach."

Immediately, I knew she was right. Faith leaped back up in my heart. Here was a beautiful chance for commitment to work in an emergency. I knew it would either work, or I would be faced with the costly prospect of paying one house payment in Charlotte and another in California.

Tammy and I prayed. "Lord, we commit this problem to you. If that house doesn't sell and if we can't make the payments, we might have to go to the poorhouse, but you're going with us. This is your problem and we give it to you."

That night we went to bed and slept like babies.

Twenty-four hours later, I received a call from California. The house had been resold for several thousand dollars more than I had paid for it. Commitment had won again!

Once you've committed a situation to God, rest your case with Him. It's like a case being tried in court. After the pros and cons of a case have been explained before a judge, the case is rested. Then the jury brings its verdict. That's exactly what you're doing with your problems. Rest your case with God. Let Him bring the answer to pass. Let Him bring the solution to you. He will care for you and show you exactly what to do.

Many times even after we've committed that nagging problem to God, the answer somehow seems stalled. There are occasions when we've told the Lord the problem was His, yet within moments we are still mentally working the situation out. Does that sound familiar?

Sometimes commitment has to be a moment-by-moment experience. Otherwise things like anxiety, worry, and fear can stall the answer. Problems can easily entangle us unless commitment becomes a lifestyle, a way of living for us.

"Casting all your anxiety upon him, because he cares for you" says the Scripture in 1 Peter 5:7 (NAS). The word *cast* means "to throw," like tossing a ball. If we actually trust Jesus, then it's time to throw Him the ball. Throw the problem to Him.

Keep your eyes on Jesus even as you commit the problem of survival to Him and look for the answer from Him. Hebrews 12:1 (NAS) gives us some sound advice for handling our nagging problems of stalled commitment. "Let us also lay aside every encumbrance, and the sin which so easily entangles us, and let us run with endurance the race that is set before us, fixing our eyes on Jesus, the author and perfector of faith."

We must remind ourselves again and again of what Jesus said in Matthew 12:25, "And Jesus knew their thoughts and said unto them, Every kingdom divided against itself is brought to desolation; and every city or house divided against itself shall not stand." If we're going to have power, we must have unity. We've got to be of one mind, in one accord, if we're going to see the power of God demonstrated in this generation.

We're going to have to totally commit ourselves to God and resist the devil and together go forward and win the world to Jesus Christ. Once again we must remind ourselves and hear the cry of Moses as he cried to the children of Israel, "Who is on the Lord's side? Who is on the Lord's side?" We must stand up right now. We must stand up and be counted. We must shout it from the roof tops, from the street corners, in the morning and at noon and at night: "I am on the Lord's side! I am on the Lord's side! I'm in the army of the almighty God and I am more than a conqueror through Jesus Christ."

Yes, we have the power of the Holy Ghost. We have the tools of the Gospel. We have the greatest and finest facilities for taking the world for Jesus Christ. Now is the time we must gear ourselves to win the world. It is time to unite and go forth.

As we consider the prophecies of the Word of God, we see that we are in the very last hours of time. There is no doubt about it. All the prophets today are crying out that the time is short. Jesus is coming. Jesus is coming soon for His Bride. If we have any good intentions of getting into the army of God and doing something for Him, we must do it now or forget it. Yes, we must stand up and be counted.

7

Give
a Good Report

If Christians are ever going to unite, we must
walk in the reality that the Holy Spirit has revealed to
us, and we must confess it with our lips.

Romans 10:9 tells us that if we confess with our mouth
the Lord Jesus Christ and shall believe in our hearts
that God has raised Him from the dead, then we will be
saved. You see, we must put our belief into action, and
one sure way of doing this is to speak out the truth.

Jesus says in Luke 6:45, "A good man out of the good
treasure of his heart bringeth forth that which is good;
and an evil man out of the evil treasure of his heart
bringeth forth that which is evil: for of the abundance of
the heart his mouth speaketh."

Your future, your success, your testimony, your very
life is governed by what you speak. Proverbs 18:21 says,
"Death and life are in the power of the tongue." If we are
ever going to unite as the Body of Christ, we *must* speak
it out!

Speech is undoubtedly one of the most powerful forces on this earth. God, Himself, spoke the entire universe into being. In creation, He gave man the power to speak and the ability to choose what to say, whether good or evil. While our speech is by choice, for a Christian a good confession is not an option; it is a necessity.

The thing that has often kept Christianity back from success and total victory in this world is a bad and negative confession by both our actions and our speech.

We have all met people, even in our churches, who are always negative: their kids are sick; their job is rotten; this has gone wrong; the weather is bad; they always seem miserable. Their own confession has put them in a negative realm in which they will stay until they confess God's Word and give a good report.

Each of us has the opportunity to change our life by what we speak. Matthew 12:37 says that by our words, we will be justified or condemned. In fact, Jesus, in the same conversation, says that a Christian can be known by the fruit of his lips just as a good tree is known by its fruit. Therefore, I really question whether a person is a Christian who is negative all the time.

For many, their degree of success, the condition of their home, their family, their business, and their health is a direct result of their confession. And I believe the future of the Church also lies in what we confess. We can confess doom or prosperity.

Doctors have learned recently that our body will work to keep us honest to our confession. If we confess fear, our body responds and produces it, sometimes to the point of heart failure (Luke 21:26). If we confess complaints and bitterness, our body will produce it in arthritis, cancer, etc. However, we can also confess a good report, and our body will produce healing, life, and prosperity. So it is with the Body of Christ.

Proverbs 15:30, one of Henry Harrison's (my co-host) favorite Scriptures says, "A good report makes the bones fat." The Hebrew literally says, "A good report refreshes the whole body and causes the whole body to prosper." This is not only true in the physical realm but also in the spiritual. As we give a good report, a good testimony, we help the whole Body of Christ.

I believe this is the reason that God has so blessed PTL's venture into 24 hours-a-day satellite broadcasting around the world. Instead of beaming violence and evil, it is airing a good report of Christian testimony and music 24 hours a day, not just using PTL's programs, but programs from all the leading Christian ministries, all working together, causing the whole Body to prosper.

God loves a good report. Hebrews, chapter 11, is like a Christian "Hall of Fame." It is a record of those men that gave a good report (vs 39) and who confessed they were looking for a better land (vs 14). For most, their circumstances were worse than yours or mine, but because they gave a good report, God honored them above measure.

The book of Job is a clear testimony of how to get out of a bad situation by giving a good report. If there ever was a situation where a person had a right to give a bad report, it was Job's. God tested Job by allowing the devil to afflict him, so even his wife suggested he "curse God and die." But the Bible says that Job did not sin with his lips. He could look in faith beyond his present adverse circumstances to see in nature and his own experience God's greatness and goodness. So when Job prayed for his three backbiting neighbors, God restored all his blessings and made Job the most blessed man on earth at that time.

Our present bad situation may be trying to keep us from making a good confession. Forget the circumstances; let's look up to God. The Bible says, "Let the weak say, I am strong" (Joel 3:10). We can change our husband or wife, our business, our chruch, our pastor, all by a good confession. Just as we see everything in the Bible is positive when we see it in its proper context, all things are working together for our good when we confess good things.

Hebrews 10:23 tells us "to hold fast to our profession of faith without wavering." That means we must speak it forth. I enjoy sharing my faith in Jesus everyday on national television because I know as I confess Christ, He is confessing me before the Father.

Just as God loves a good report, He hates an evil report. We can see this clearly in God's Word. In Numbers 13, we see the children of Israel preparing to cross Jordan to go over to the promised land. But Moses, first, sends twelve spies into the land to bring back a report. When they return, ten of the twelve bring back an evil report. Instead of confessing God's power and the goodness of the land, they speak of giants, walled cities, and great enemies in the land (vs 32).

What was the result of their evil report? The Israelites started murmuring against God and decided that slavery in Egypt would be better, even after they had seen so many miracles of God.

There are churches today that have been wiped out or have fallen into spiritual bondage by one evil report, gossip, or backbiting. God was so upset with the spies' evil report that He determined to smite them with pestilence and disinherit them. Those who gave the evil report indeed died on the spot by a plague (Numbers

14:37). A plague of death also fell upon Ananias and Sapphira in Acts 5 because of their sinful, lying confession, despite the fact they had done a good deed.

What about the two spies, Joshua and Caleb, who gave the good report? Because of their positive trusting confession, they were almost stoned by a mob of their own people. But God honored them and promised that they alone of their whole generation would enter and possess the promised land (Numbers 14:24). God honored their *confession* of faith as a title deed to Canaan, more than if they had worked years to earn it.

Today, God will honor our confession of faith in the same way. When God gave us the idea for Heritage Village, we had no money and no visible means to get any. But we confessed it before God and man, and God has honored that confession. Today, Heritage Village is built and totally paid for.

If we as Christians only knew the power we have in our tongue to produce life, prosperity, and Christian victory, I believe we would take the world for Christ this very year. John, in Revelation, chapter 12, saw the devil cast out of heaven to earth to try to deceive the saints. But the saints overcame him! How? By the blood of the Lamb and the word of their testimony!

We don't have to fight the devil. We have more power on the tip of our tongue than the whole devil's army. All we have to do is confess God's Word and tell the devil to get lost. First John 4:4 says, "Greater is he that is in you, than he that is in the world." We are more than conquerors in Jesus. Whosoever is born of God overcomes the world (1 John 5:4).

This is our good report. This is the confession that is bigger than any problem the enemy can throw at us. As we confess God's goodness and power and love, it is our title to success and every one of God's promises and privileges in His Kingdom. We can unite in the truth that the Holy Spirit has revealed to us as we confess it with our lips.

8

The Hour
of the CHURCH

There is mounting fear and anxiety in our nation as perhaps never before in our history. Our President has termed it a "crisis in confidence," but there is a questioning, a concern, a lack of trust in our political leaders, in our government, in our school, in our businesses, and in ourselves. People are worried about all kinds of shortages and are asking, "What can be done?"

Certainly, the problem is not isolated in America. As I have traveled outside of America, I have seen the shortages; the unrest of the people is even more pronounced. People everywhere are looking for some kind of answers, and there are plenty of opinions and theories around today.

However, I believe the answer to our questions and every problem we face in life is the Bible rather than the experts. Just months ago, all the experts predicted that

PTL would fall from attacks of certain people and because of some money problems; but God said, "No weapon formed against thee shall prosper." PTL has not only survived; it has thrived and grown during this time. Yes, God's Word has the answer!

The Bible says much about the days in which we are living. It tells about the perilous times we're facing. In Matthew 24, Jesus described a series of events before His Second Coming that reads like today's headlines. God tells us that He will not wink at sin and look the other way forever. From the beginning, God warned that His Spirit would not always strive with man. What a man sows, that also shall he reap (Gal. 6:7).

I believe we are in the hour of coming judgment and final preparation of the Church. Our history is rushing to a climax, and there are a lot of people who deep down inside want to become a part of the family of God and Body of Christ but think they can wait until the last minute. For some, the events of today are going to pass them by, and it's going to be too late for them. Some will harden their hearts, and as the Bible says, "They will be cut off and that without remedy" (Prov. 29:1).

Even churches can harden their hearts. As a member of the spiritual life committee for my particular denomination, I was asked to write down alarming trends I saw in the Body of Christ. One of those I saw was that our great churches can easily become impersonal to people's needs. People that are confused and hurting are getting lost in the crowd. What they really need are friends—people to put their arms around them and touch the hurts with love and compassion.

The other alarming trend, the great breakdown of the home and divorce, reveals the same need for closeness and communication. The same Gospel that works in great charismatic meetings must work down in the trenches, in our homes on a day-to-day level. And it will if we let it. Jesus says, "I am touched by the feelings of your infirmities." He is a friend that is closer than a brother. When you hurt, He hurts.

Our God is a God of detail, and He is concerned about each thing down to the number of hairs on our head.

God says the way the Church will survive today's calamities is to fellowship and care for one another. If we just come and sit in a pew and don't relate and minister to one another, we'll miss the fullness of what God has for the Church today.

So many people are attracted to the meetings with the great healers. The sick want to be touched by the great ministers. In actuality, if the truth was published, the prayer phone ministry of PTL would probably be known as one of the great healing ministries of the world today. Our counselors are praying with people and seeing miracles every day, but I don't want to propagate our ministry that way. I prefer to be recognized only as a part of the Body of Christ because the day of the great single preacher or healer is drawing to a close.

This is the hour of the Church, the Body of Christ. God is saying to every pastor, every church member, "Be filled with the Holy Spirit." Each of us should pray for the sick and minister to one another's needs, for it is the whole Church that is going to rise triumphant at His Coming!

The only way the whole Church can get prepared is if all the members minister to one another. There are only so many people that I or anyone can preach to personally, and even then I can easily fail. It is a rude awakening for many in the Church to see their "preacher idols" as imperfect people just as they themselves are.

No one preacher is going to do the whole job, even for his own church. Somehow, even if he could, I don't believe God would let him.

Today we are on the brink of events that require every part of the Body of Christ to join in and help. What if the government decides to pull the plug on Christian television (and there are those who now want this)? What if a power failure or shortage limits use of television to bare necessities? Who is going to come to your home to minister to you? There is only One who can—that One, of course, is JESUS.

Jesus will come in your brother or neighbor. God has always chosen to use men and women. We are all the arms and legs He's got. He's not going to use the angels to evangelize and love, for He has said, "I've chosen you." In that calling, He charges us to pray for one another, to read the Bible together, to care for one another and share our needs and blessings together.

The days reveal it, the Spirit confirms it, and we all know it: Jesus is coming soon!

In the midst of crises and falling away, Jesus, the Good Shepherd, is gathering together all the true believers in His flock. Do you know that we, the Church, are God's most prized possession on earth—that we are gifts in which God delights? When we ignore or hurt one another, we are messing with a gift of God. We are precious to God, but our neighbors are just as precious. Each one of us needs to discern and recognize the Body of Christ.

The hardest statement for me to hear from a Christian is for them to say, "Nobody cares." This is a poor commentary on the Body of Christ. We had better care. We *are* our brother's keeper, and though we may not think we need the Body of Christ, one of these days everyone of us will need it.

I like to preach about victory. I'm not a preacher of doom and gloom, but I cannot ignore the warning of God's Word. Second Timothy 3:1 says, "This know also, that in the last days perilous times shall come," and already we see them all around us. When the world leaders start talking about Armageddon (and most of them don't even understand what it is), something is happening!

When I was a kid, people used to wonder what could possibly happen to cause such a monstrous war as Armageddon. Today we know the cause—the world is being strangled by the need for oil. Countries can be literally ground to a halt without oil. In our own country, if we run out of oil, it's all over.

How do you operate a 100-story skyscraper without electricity? These buildings are sealed so they have to have air conditioning and lights. Our whole automobile industry is dependent on fuel, and if it dies, the economy of our whole nation is gone because so many industries are interrelated.

Can you tell me that when one nation has a stranglehold on the very substance which others need to stay alive that there will not be war? The Bible says that the mighty bear, Russia, will come down and that the Arab oil will not lie untouched forever.

With or without oil, experts are saying that inflation has so escalated in our nation that we are on a crash course to disaster. In his book, Robert Preston says that the results of the coming economic collapse will be millions out of work, literal starvation, and rioting and looting that will sweep the nation.

Willard Cantelon, the great student of world finance, says the end of the dollar is near.

David Wilkerson says famine is coming to the world in our generation, and millions will die.

Dr. Paul Yurich of Stanford University confirms that as many as 20 million people will die of starvation in the coming year.

Jesus, Himself, told us that famine is a sign of the last days. So what will you do, what will be your security when you are faced with no job, no food, and worthless money? The Bible tells us in Proverbs 11:4, "Riches profit not in the day of wrath: but righteousness delivereth from death."

The wealthy are not necessarily the ones who will make it during the times of tribulation and hunger. In verse 28 of that same chapter, Solomon declares, "He that trusteth in his riches shall fall: but the righteous shall flourish as a branch."

Some of you can remember the last depression we had in this country. Who were the people who jumped out of windows and committed suicide? It was those who put all their hopes and faith in money and stocks and bonds. When their god of money failed, they couldn't exist.

During depression and hard times, the most fortunate are the poor. They hardly know the difference. I remember as a lad, my family, grandparents, and relatives never went hungry during the depression. They had always shared food and took care of each other. The believers in our little church pitched in, and there was always enough to go around.

God has got a secret weapon against depression. It is the Body of Christ. One of my favorite Scriptures, Psalm 37:3, declares that if we trust in the Lord, "Verily, thou shalt be *fed*." At the bottom line, food is what it takes to survive. During the coming days, the Church of Jesus Christ will not wring its hands, worrying about what is going to happen. Rather the Church is going to rise up triumphant as the day of redemption draws near.

God surely has the days and the times in His control, but we must heed the warning of the Bible. It was a little widow woman that God sent to Elijah to feed him during the time of famine in his day, and God is going to use the widow woman and the whole Body of Christ as your provision in the coming days. When the bottom falls out, you may need the help and knowledge of the older people who know how to garden and farm and sew.

This is not a message of discouragement, but it is Bible and God's word for *now*—that God's people must come together and care and help one another. The true New Testament Church is a loving and caring Body of believers.

If the Church today was really doing all it could, there would be no need for welfare in America. The needs of the congregation would be administered in a spirit of love, and the orphans and widows would be cared for as God says they should. Instead, we've given the government more and more control until we've got a monster that has shifted our dependence on God over to man.

The New Testament Church cared and shared. Acts 2:44-46 records:

And all that believed were together, and had all things common; and sold their possessions and goods, and parted them to all men, as every man had need. And they, continuing daily with one accord in the temple, and breaking bread from house to house, did eat their meat with gladness and singleness of heart.

We may need this same New Testament formula in the Church today if Jesus tarries, and that could be a blessing. While we need individual motivation and responsibility, I don't believe God ever intended us to live such high-geared lives with so much pressure to perform and produce. This is why so many today are having nervous breakdowns. Rather, God says that we are to cast our care on Him and rest in Him.

The carnal man could never equally share and work together without destroying one another. But motivated by love, the Church *can* according to 1 Corinthians 12:25-26, "That there should be no schism in the body; but that the members should have the same care one for another. And whether one member suffer, all the members suffer with it; or one member be honored, all the members rejoice with it."

While the carnal man would get jealous with others who are blessed, we should take others' blessings in the Body as being our own family blessed; and when someone hurts, we can share that hurt by listening, consoling, and loving. If we all really cared for one another like this, I believe the Church would win millions overnight.

Today, with homosexuality rampant, the devil has most of us even afraid to express our love for one another in the Body. People are dying for lack of love and friendship; and we must not let the smokescreen, the counterfeit of Satan, keep us from attending to the real needs in our chruch.

Jesus came to heal the brokenhearted and bind up the bruised. God, today, wants each of us to befriend and help the bruised and wounded among us—to give them the "wine and oil of the Holy Spirit," that they may be restored in soul and body.

The *whole* Church in these days is going to nourish and take care of each other. That means we all have a part, a job to do. We must unite to have real life and be prepared for that soon triumphant meeting with our Lord in the air.

9

A Majority
with God

In Revelation 21:7 we read, "He that overcometh shall inherit all things; and I will be his God, and he shall be my son." Even if the odds are against us, because we are children of God, we win. And yes, my friend, you will win.

You might say, "But everything is against me. The economy is against me. Inflation is against me."

I don't care. God has a special math that doesn't have anything to do with the mathematical system of the world. If you don't believe me, read Leviticus 26:8, and you will find that it says, "And five of you shall chase an hundred, and an hundred of you shall put ten thousand to flight (I wonder where he went to school!): and your enemies shall fall before you by the sword." My friend, that is God's math.

God and you make a majority no matter what the odds against you are. If all are against you, God will sustain you and He will lift you up. "For if God be for us, who can be against us" (Rom. 8:31). "Greater is he that is in you, than he that is in the world" (1 John 4:4). If you don't believe God's math, my friend, you had better read the Book over and over and over again.

How many did Gideon have in his army? Three hundred and one—the General. Three hundred and one. History tell us that from three hundred thousand to one and one-half million people were slain by the three hundred in Gideon's army. Oh, but you might add, "I'm only one." No, remember again that one with God is a majority.

Every time I'm around Oral Roberts it seems I slip and say something like, "But I don't have a degree from a place like O.R.U."

He looks at me with a stern look and a father's voice and says, "Jim Bakker, stop that! Don't ever confess that! With God you can do all things!"

"But, Oral, I'm only 5'8".

Again Oral chuckles and says, "Jim, I'm not as big as Billy Graham. He's real tall. But then you come along and you're short. So you see, we balance each other, don't we?"

In reading the story of David, I began to wonder if I had ever seen a real tall Jewish person. And I had to realize that I hadn't seen too many. Yet, that little Jewish boy, that boy named David, went out to face the giant. How could he do it?

You say, "I've got giants in my business. There are giants in the church. I've got giant problems. There are giants confronting me everywhere. And I don't know what to do about it."

Well, David faced that giant. But he used God's math. The Bible doesn't tell us that David just went out to battle. He just didn't walk onto the field. The Bible says that David *ran* to the giant. He ran to the roar. Why? Because he had God's math working for him.

Tammy recently published a book called *Run To The Roar*. We have discovered in our lives that Satan is as "a roaring lion, seeking whom he may devour." But because of Jesus Christ and the Cross of Calvary and the resurrection, he has had his teeth pulled and he's harmless. We need to run toward him with the power of God and watch him flee.

What about those Hebrew children who were thrown into the fiery furnace? Those poor Hebrew children. The King was against them; the army was against them; it seemed like everybody was against them. But there they were: Shadrach, Meshach, and Abednego. They stood even against the government of that day. (I might add, when a government is against God, we must, as they did, put God first. He has to be first.)

Because of their determination to stand alone with God, they were thrown into that furnace which had been prepared for them and was fired up seven times hotter than before. It was so hot that the soldiers who threw them in were burned to death. But the strangest thing happened! As the three children of Israel were thrown into the furnace, they didn't burn! And as they looked into the furnace, they saw a fourth man. And He looked like the Son of God.

Yes, with God we can withstand the fiery furnaces of Satan's trial. One with God is a majority!

Daniel had found favor in the sight of Darius the king. As a matter of fact, he was preferred above the presidents and princes. This was because of the excellent spirit that was within him. Consequently, these presidents and princes wanted to bring Daniel down. They made a new law that whoever asked a petition for thirty days to any man save the king would be cast into the den of lions. King Darius signed the decree.

Even though Daniel knew the decree had been signed, he went into his house, and with his windows wide open, he still knelt three times a day and prayed and gave thanks to his God. And the men caught him in the act of praying. Then they took this before the king. The king realized he had been deceived and tricked, and he wanted to overrule his decree. But he also knew that the law of the Medes and Persians was that no decree or law which had been established could be changed. And they took Daniel and cast him into the lions' den.

The king even said unto Daniel, "Thy God whom thou serveth continually—He will deliver thee." The king sealed the mouth of the den with his ring. And the king, because of the torment within him, could not sleep. He spent the night fasting and praying.

The next morning when he arose very early, he went with haste to the den of lions. The king shouted, "Oh, Daniel, Daniel, servant of the living God, is thy God whom thou servest continually able to deliver thee from the lions?"

Then Daniel said to the king, "Oh, King, live forever. My God sent His angel and has shut the lions' mouths. They have not hurt me."

And the king honored God and made a new law. "In every dominion of my kingdom men tremble and fear before the God of Daniel: for he is the living God, and stedfast forever, and his kingdom that which shall not be destroyed, and his dominion shall be even unto the end. He delivereth and rescueth, and he worketh signs and wonders in heaven and in earth, who hath delivered

Daniel from the power of the lions."

And, my friends, that is the same God that we serve today. He still works signs and wonders in heaven and in earth, and He will deliver all of us from the power of Satan if we only submit to Him. He has given us all power in heaven and in earth because of His Son Jesus.

The odds certainly were against Daniel, but he won because of his position in God.

Elijah was a man who also faced great odds when he confronted a back-slidden king and godless priests.

King Ahab was a man who did evil in the sight of the Lord. He raised an altar for Baal in Samaria. The Scripture tells us that King Ahab did more to provoke the Lord of Israel to anger than all the kings of Israel that were before him.

Then we have Elijah coming upon the scene to bring the children of Israel to repentance. You will remember how Elijah prayed that it would not rain for 3½ years. Needless to say, things must have gotten pretty rough on the land of Israel to be in drought that long.

Ahab sent Obadiah, a man who really feared the Lord, out to look for water and green grass for the cattle before everything died. They divided the kingdom in half—Ahab was going to cover half of it and Obadiah the other half. Along the way Obadiah ran into Elijah. Elijah told him to go tell Ahab to come and see him. Of course, without the protection of God this meant death; for Ahab, needless to say, was angry at Elijah.

It wasn't long until the two of them met. Ahab said to Elijah, "Are you the one who has brought this trouble upon Israel?"

Isn't that very typical? Rather than examining ourselves, we are always trying to put the blame on someone else. Well, Elijah wasn't going to take the blame. He said, "I haven't caused any trouble for Israel. But you and your father's house have forsaken the commandments of the LORD and have followed Baal; that's why the trouble is upon the land."

Then Elijah told Ahab to gather all of Israel and come to the mount of Carmel. He told him to bring the prophets of Baal, which numbered about 450, and the prophets of the groves, about 400, which ate at Jezebel's table.

So Ahab did what was requested and sent out unto all the children of Israel and gathered the prophets together unto Mount Carmel. Elijah came to the people and very boldly (remember this is one against 850) said, "How long are you going to halt between two opinions? if the LORD be God, follow him: but if Baal, then follow him."

And that's the call that's going forth today. Who is on the Lord's side? Come over here. Don't falter between two opinions. Serve God or serve Satan, but don't stay lukewarm.

And the people, the Scripture tells us in 1 Kings 18, stood there and answered them not a word. They were silent because of their sin.

Elijah said, "I'm only one who remains the prophet of the LORD, but Baal has 450 here. So let's put God to the test." He told them to bring forth two bulls and to let the priests have one and cut it into pieces and lay it on the wood and put no fire under it. Also, Elijah would dress the other one, lay it on the wood, and put no fire under it. He told them they could call on the name of their gods, and he would call on the name of the Lord God that answers by fire and let Him be God.

The people agreed that that would be a good test. The prophets of Baal dressed their bull, put it on the altar, and from morning until noon called unto Baal. But there was no voice, no answer. They even jumped upon their altar and yelled.

By this time Elijah started mocking them. He told them to cry louder, for their god might be talking or pursuing, or he was on a journey, or maybe he was asleep and they must awaken him. The prophets of Baal screamed and cut themselves until the blood literally gushed out of them. Then evening came upon them, and still there had been no word spoken from their god Baal.

Then Elijah spoke again and told all the people to come near to him. And he prepared the altar of the Lord that was broken down. He took twelve stones according to the number of the tribes of Jacob. He built an altar in the name of the Lord. He made a trench around the altar big enough to contain two measures of seed. He put the wood in order, cut his bull in pieces, and laid it on the wood. He said, "Fill four barrels with water, and pour it on the burnt sacrifice, and on the wood." And then, as though that was not enough, he told them to do it again and then a third time. And the water ran off around the altar and filled the trench that he had dug with water.

And when it was time for the offering of the evening sacrifice, Elijah stood before the altar and said, "LORD God of Abraham, Isaac, and of Israel, let it be known this day that thou art God in Israel, and that I am thy servant, and that I have done all these things at thy word. Hear me, O LORD, hear me, that this people may know that thou art the LORD God, and that thou hast turned their heart back again."

And instantly, "the fire of the LORD fell, and consumed the burnt sacrifice, and the wood, and the stone, and the dust, and licked up the water that was in the trench. And when the people saw it, they fell on their

110/SURVIVAL: Unite to Live

faces: and said, the LORD, he is the God; the LORD, he is the God."

Elijah then slew the prophets of Baal, and it began to rain. Today, as never before, we stand at the very threshold of rain. Today, as never before, we stand at the very threshold of the experience that Elijah had on Mt. Carmel. Today we see so many of God's children tossed to and fro by every wind of doctrine, and they're haulted between two opinions. We must realize that if God is God, He will take care of us and He will vindicate Himself. We must walk in the reality that one with God is a majority.

Elijah knew his God. It didn't make any difference to him if he was one against 850, and he knew that he could take care of any situation with both hands tied behind his back because he knew God.

Elijah had power in his prayers, and he knew that he was in a position to expect an answer. I can just imagine those backslidden Israelites hanging around saying, as he dumped the water on the sacrfice, "Be careful, the day of miracles might be past. Maybe something by accident could get the fire going; oh, but Elijah, you're such an idiot, now you're drenching it with water. There is no way that that is going to burn." But, praise God, Elijah knew his God, and he knew that God and one were a majority.

Not only was the offering consumed, but everything around the altar was consumed. When God does something, He does it in absolute perfection. This is what God wants to do for every one of you. This is what God has done for us at PTL. Yes, the enemy did come in like a flood. The enemy came in with everything it had and tried to invade us with a flood. But, praise God, the Scripture tells us that when Satan comes in like a flood,

God will lift up His hand against him.

In 1979 the government came in, and streams of debt moved in—every harassment that possibly could, happened to us—it all moved in at the same time. On top of that, some psychic magazine predicted that I would go under. I really needed that, when at that time I was 13 million dollars behind in bills.

Many of my Christian friends had turned on me, the government had turned on me, and then this psychic magazine had a horoscope that lashed out against PTL and predicted the very month we would go under. Then the magazine hedged a little bit and said, "Well, if he doesn't go under during that month, by two months later (that would be September of 1979) PTL will be but a memory in America." Praise God, we are still here and growing as never before.

You know what the outcome of that prediction was? The very month that the prophets of Satan predicted PTL's collapse, God had me challenge them over national TV that this would not happen and that they would be the ones that would be destroyed.

And when I did that, Satan whispered in my ear, "Jim Bakker, you're a fool. What if it doesn't happen and you *do* go under. You'll discredit the whole kingdom of God. You're stupid to stick your neck out, Jim Bakker."

And God said to me, "Jim, you're not sticking your neck out; your sticking *My* neck out, and no one is going to cut *My* head off." Yes, I challenged the prophet of Baal, and I stated the God whom I served, the God of Abraham, Isaac, and Jacob, would deliver me. And the very month that they said we'd go under was the biggest month in the history of PTL. We received almost seven million dollars in income and won more souls to Jesus Christ that month than ever in our history.

The editor of that psychic magazine wondered who was this "Joseph's boy," this little boy who was challenging him in his psychic prediction. What in the world was I doing? Well, you know he tuned into PTL Club to find out what in the world was going on, and that was his big mistake. Because as he watched the program, the Spirit of God got a hold of his heart, and he called the prayer line and accepted Jesus Christ as his personal Saviour. And not only that, but the very month that he prophesied that we would go under, the Lord had him close down his magazine, and by the end of summer, that magazine was a memory. His word had boomeranged, and the prophecy came back on him. But, praise God, he now knows Jesus, and he knows the God of Abraham, Isaac, and Jacob Who lives today.

Today as the army of Jesus Christ goes forth, we must stand up. We must not be weak, mamby pamby members of the Body of Christ anymore. We must stand up to do as it says in James 4:7, "Submit yourselves therefore to God. (Then) resist the devil, and he will flee from you." Yes, that's you, my brother and sister, that's you. Resist the devil, and he will flee from you. You as a child of God have more power in your little finger than the devil has in his whole being.

If Spirit-filled Christians ever *really* discover that, they're going to be doubly dangerous to Satan. Many of you are saying, "How do we achieve the impossible? Jim, what you're sharing with us here in this book might work for you, but it's impossible for me." My friend, I want to tell you something, if Jim Bakker can do it, you can do it. God wants you to trust Him.

10

The Lord Is on Our Side

Many times in our Christian lives we seem to come to an impasse. Maybe you've been trying to love a neighbor, and they've misunderstood your motives and turned against you. Perhaps you've been trying to keep your family together and something has come along to destroy all you've tried to do. Or perhaps sickness has entered your life and you have just been so discouraged.

In my own life I've come to impasses where I would wonder if I was going to survive. Will we get the necessary money? Will the permit be approved? Will we be able to go on?

But in all this I've discovered a tremendous truth from the Word that gives me the courage to go on—**God is on our side**. Tammy Faye has been singing a song the last few weeks that all America is going to be singing, if they're not already. It's called "If It Had Not Been For The Lord On My Side."

It seems that anyone with vision—anyone who sticks his head above the crowd to try something—is going to have some opposition. There are forces that will try to stop a person with vision, whether that vision is to win your mate to Christ or to have enough money to support your family or to build Heritage Village.

Whenever the opposition comes, we can go to Psalm 118:6 and read the vibrant truth, "The Lord is on my side!" That's right, the Word declares that the Lord is on our side.

I've heard so many people over the years say, "It's not God being on my side; it's my being on God's side that counts." And it is important that we are on God's side. But, praise God, the Bible says that God is already on *our* side. God is not only my God and Jesus Christ, my Savior; but Jesus is also my elder brother, according to Romans 8:29. And that means I have a big Brother, and the opposition better not pick on me because my big Brother will come and fight my battles for me.

Psalm 118 continues, "I will not fear: what can man do unto me? The LORD taketh my part with them that help me." Imagine that, not only is the Lord on our side, but He will bless those who help us.

The Scripture continues, "Therefore shall I see my desire upon them that hate me. It is better to trust in the LORD than to put confidence in man. It is better to trust in the LORD than to put confidence in princes." With God on our side *we win.*

My four-year-old son Jamie has heard me talk about Jesus many times and has heard me give hundreds of invitations for people to accept Jesus Christ, and not long ago he asked his mother, "Mommie, how do I accept Jesus Christ? I want to ask Jesus into my heart."

Little Jamie listened to Tammy as she explained to

him how to pray and ask Jesus to come into his heart. And then he looked up and said, "Mommie, is Jesus in my heart now?"

Tammy gently responded, "Yes, if you've asked Him in, He's come in."

Jamie stopped and tightened his jaw in a closed position and looked up to Tammy and said between his teeth, "I'm going to keep my mouth shut so He can't get out."

Praise God, Jesus won't leave us that easy. I believe so many people have gotten the mistaken idea that God is against them . . . that God somehow is a God who wants to send judgment on them . . . that somehow God is a God who is up there on a throne looking angry and mean and just waiting for you to do something wrong so He can club you. I know many people have been taught that kind of theology about God.

But I have news for every one of you; God is on your side. God is fighting the battles for you. God so loved you that He sent His only begotten Son to die. God is on your side today.

Romans 8:31 says, "What shall we then say to these things. If God be for us, who can be against us?" God is for you! You! I want you to accept the fact that God is on your side. Here's what the Scripture says. "If God be for us (then God *is* for us), who can be against us?"

Ephesians 2:4-5 states, "But God, who is rich in mercy, for his great love wherewith he loved us, even when we were dead in sins, hath quickened us (made us alive) together with Christ. By grace are ye saved." Even when we were dead in sin, Christ loved us. I believe, and many people are shaken up when I say this, that God is even on the side of the sinner. Many people don't understand that. God made you. God created you.

And God is for you. God is for you. We can agree with 1 John 4:19, "We love him, because he first loved us."

The Word of God tells us that the Lord is even married to the backslider. Jeremiah 3:14 says, "Turn, O backsliding children, saith the LORD; for I am married unto you."

So many people think that the devil's on their side. Many have the mistaken idea that when they serve the devil, the devil's going to give them some benefits. But I know differently. You can be on the devil's side, but the devil will never be on your side. The devil will *never* be on your side. God can be on your side and God *is* on your side, but the devil is not on your side because he's a con man. He's a deceiver. He is the father of lies.

He has lied to millions of people, and they think if they turn their lives over to the devil, he will bless them somehow. But, in the end, the devil destroys everyone who serves him. So the devil's never on your side. You can be on the devil's side, but he'll never be on your side. That is for sure. The devil is your enemy.

First Peter 5:8 says,"Be sober, be vigilant; because your adversary the devil (he's your adversary), as a roaring lion, walketh about, seeking whom he may devour." The devil's job is to destroy.

John 10:10 firmly states, "The thief cometh not, but for to steal, and to kill, and to destroy. I am come that they might have life, and that they might have it more abundantly." The devil's job is to destroy. But God said Jesus came that we might have life and that we might have it more abundantly.

I want you to know today that the Lord is on your side. He's on your side right now no matter what you're facing. God wants you to come through in victory. You may be going through the most difficult time of your life. You may be facing surgery. You may be facing a very big bill. You may have some past-due bills. You may have a marriage problem. You may have a college problem. You may have a relationship problem with your other family members. You may have a child on drugs. And you may be saying, "There's no hope for me. I'm going through deep water. I'm going through a problem. I don't know which way to turn."

I want to tell you today that God's on your side. God will deliver you. Don't look to the left. Don't look to the right. But look to God because God is here to take care of your need today.

The song "If It Had Not Been For The Lord On My Side" was taken from Psalm 124. If you're going through deep water, or you know somebody that's going through deep water, I want you to know that God will bring you through. Here are the exact words of the psalm where the song came from.

If it had not been the LORD who was on our side, now may Israel say;
If it had not been the LORD who was on our side, when men rose up against us:
Then they had swallowed us up quick, when their wrath was kindled against us:
Then the waters had overwhelmed us, the stream had gone over our soul:
Then the proud waters had gone over our soul. Blessed be the LORD, who hath not given us as a prey to their teeth.
Our soul is escaped as a bird out of the snare of the fowlers: the snare is broken, and we are escaped.
Our help is in the name of the LORD, who made heaven and earth.

The psalmist David cried out, "Oh, Lord, they would overwhelm me. They came in like a flood. They were like the waters that were deep. I was in deep trouble. But, God, you were on my side. And you delivered me."

I want you to know that if you're living and breathing, God's on your side. God wants to deliver you more than you want deliverance. God wants to bless you more than you want to be blessed. God is on your side this day. You may be going through some deep water, but if you will stick with God's Word—stay with it, live in it—it will bring you out of the trial victoriously.

The Word tells us that our trials are more precious than gold. First Peter 1:6-7 says that you can rejoice "though now for a season, if need be, ye are in heaviness through manifold temptations. That the trial of your faith, being much more precious than of gold that perisheth, though it be tried with fire, might be found unto praise and honour and glory at the appearing of Jesus Christ." The trial of your faith is more precious than gold.

Do you know why people are living beneath their privileges today? It's because they go through trials, not understanding that they're solid gold-lined clouds—that they're solid gold trials—that if they'll begin to rejoice in that trial, if they'll stand firm in that trial, that God is going to deliver them. God is going to bring them out. And they're going to have the greatest victory they've ever known.

The founders of the *Great Passion Play* in Eureka Springs, Arkansas, could have given up when opposition formed. But, no, they said, "We have claimed the mountain. We're going to stay with it." And through the tears and trials they stood with it, and today millions of people have heard and seen the message of the Gospel of Jesus Christ. Why? Because two people stayed on the mountain and said, "We're not going to move off. We've heard from God, and the trial of our faith is going to bring us forth as pure gold."

I want you to know something. God will deliver you from all your enemies. Isaiah 41:10-13 proclaims, "Fear thou not; for I am with thee: be not dismayed; for I am thy God: I will strengthen thee; yea, I will help thee: Yea, I will uphold thee with the right hand of my righteousness. Behold, all they that were incensed against thee shall be ashamed and confounded: they shall be as nothing; and they that strive with thee shall perish. Thou shalt seek them, and shalt not find them, even them that contended with thee: they that war against thee shall be as nothing, and as a thing of naught. For I the LORD thy God will hold thy right hand, saying unto thee, Fear not; I will help thee."

Another Scripture, one that really helped me through a year-and-a-half of struggles, is Isaiah 54:17—"No weapon that is formed against thee shall prosper." And the rest of that verse goes on, "And every tongue that shall rise against thee in judgment thou shalt condemn. This is the heritage of the servants of the LORD, and their righteousness is of me, saith the LORD." He has fought our battles. No weapon formed against the children of God is going to prosper. That's His message to you. Lift your head and rejoice if you're a child of God today.

And if you're not a child of God, God is still on your side. God is waiting for you. There's still time. All you have to do is ask Him to come into your heart, and you can be on God's side—because I want you to know He's on *your* side. He loves you. He cares about you. He really does.

You know, there was a time when we were building this last year-and-a-half when I just had to stand. There are times when we don't know what to do. I went through a year-and-a-half of extreme pressure, and right in the middle of it, it looked like the devil had taken all of the imps in hell and had organized a big high-level meeting and was going to destroy me.

I had done everything I knew how to do, and now all I could do was hold on and say, "God, I did it all. I don't know what else to do." And you know what? As I stood firm, as I remained faithful and didn't move, as I stood there, God delivered me.

And I believe all Christians can do the same today. Ephesians 6:13 directs, "Wherefore take unto you the whole armour of God, that ye may be able to withstand in the evil day, and having done all, to stand." You can stand. In the midst of turmoil, when everything is falling apart around you, you can stand when you have God on your side. You can stand, knowing He is going to deliver you.

Recently I was with Robert Schuller, a good friend of mine. He was about to dedicate the Crystal Cathedral. He admitted to me that in the middle of his building program, it seemed like he wasn't going to be able to finish it. Even Robert Schuller admitted he got discouraged. Can you believe that? The minister of positive confession, one of the most positive preachers of all time, became discouraged and almost gave up.

So don't get upset if you get discouraged once in awhile. Don't berate yourself if you get down a little bit once in awhile. Just begin to read the Book and hold steady and stay faithful to God, because God's going to bring you through.

They said Robert Schuller couldn't build it. Even the

building codes said it was impossible. Yet he stayed faithful to God; he stayed with the vision, and just a few days ago one of the greatest cathedrals in the world was dedicated. Why? Because God was on his side, and he stood faithful to God.

I have noticed that whenever someone does something like build a Crystal Cathedral, the critics come out of the woodwork. You know who the critics are? They're the people who don't do anything themselves. They don't do one thing but criticize. They sit in their old moth-eaten rocking chairs and criticize everybody. It doesn't take anything to be an armchair critic. Because of the criticisms on the Crystal Cathedral, however, there's probably hardly a soul in the world who hasn't read at least one article about it and now knows what's happening.

I just got back from Hollywood, California, where Tammy was cutting her new record. While we were there, we were fortunate enough to attend a seminar on gospel music, which was sponsored by *Billboard* magazine. This was the first such seminar that *Billboard* had ever conducted. Representatives from all over the non-Christian music industry attended.

Tammy and I listened to the speakers at the opening banquet. And they told how so many secular music stores in New York had gone bankrupt, how in Detroit many record stores were going bankrupt, and how record companies themselves were going bankrupt.

The top officials in the music industry have come to the conclusion that one way to turn the record industry around is to start featuring gospel music. *Billboard* magazine is now going to devote a portion of its pages to gospel music. They want to get involved because they believe the greatest trend in coming music for the

United States of America is the gospel music.

What a turn around!

Just months ago the newspapers and reporters thought they were going to do Christians in. They began to write about Pat Robertson, they began to write about Billy Graham, they began to write about Robert Schuller, they began to write about Jerry Falwell. They put us on the covers of magazines. *Time, U.S. News,* and other magazines began to talk about the born-again movement.

But Christians began to get involved with political action and began organizing to vote their convictions. The world was all upset and began to talk about it and write about it. The government began to investigate us, and they tried to find something wrong with us.

But the more they talked, the more we grew. The more they investigated, the stronger we became. And what looked like a negative where many Christians would want to get in their churches and hide from it all, what looked like the greatest onslaught against Christianity in American history, has boomeranged on the devil. And now there are more born-again people in America than ever before.

Over fifty percent of the adult population in America now confesses to be born-again. What's happening? What's going on? God is on our side. Jesus is coming again. The Lord is taking the negative criticism and is building His Church bigger than ever. God is on your side, friend. No weapon formed against you is going to prosper.

On my way home from Hollywood I stopped to see Oral Roberts. While we chatted, Oral confessed to me that this last year has indeed been a rough one. But, you know, he kept on building. There were even some days when all he could do was simply hold on. He's now over half way through with the City of Faith, which will be the largest medical center of its kind in the world.

When I look at Oral and study his great walk of faith, I say to myself, "If Oral can survive, I can survive." And, friend, if I can survive, you can survive. I want you to know that God can meet your need.

My need is a million dollars a week. That's all. It takes a million dollars (or more) each week for me to stay on the air. And many of you have needs too. It might be a thousand dollars or a hundred dollars or any other kind of need—perhaps a marriage need or a physical need. And your need is just as big to you (or bigger) as my need is. But I know this—if God can meet my need, if God can meet Oral Roberts' need, then God's going to bring you through, too. God is no respecter of persons.

Margaret Douroux, who wrote "We're Blest," also wrote Tammy's new song "If It Had Not Been For The Lord On My Side." The reason she can write songs like that is because she has gone through the fire.

When I was in Hollywood, I did an interview with her in front of her father's church. She told of all the opposition they had encountered when they tried to build the church. Some wanted it on a different street corner; some didn't want it at all. And for about a year-and-a-half all they got up was the church walls. Nobody would loan them the money to complete the project. And there it sat with no roof!

You know, when something is only half finished, the critics really start talking. All the "I told you so's" really tell you so then. But when I interviewed Margaret, we were standing in front of the completed building.

God had brought them through. About five years ago

they completed the building. Her father had faith even when everything was seemingly falling apart and people were laughing at him. Even when they couldn't get the roof on, her father held fast and he stood.

That's why when Margaret was watching PTL Club one day, she could write the song "If It Had Not Been For The Lord On My Side."

She said, "Jim, as I saw you there with that half-finished auditorium for a year-and-a-half, all I could think about was my dad. He had a church with no roof on it, and you had a church with no walls in it." And she said, "You know, God brought my dad through, and I knew God was going to bring you through." And she sat down and penned the words, "If it had not been for the Lord on my side, oh, Lord, where would I be?"

Thank God He's on our side. Thank God that at PTL the Lord's been on our side. We had the atheists against us all at once. We had the soothsaying magazine prophesy my doom a couple of years ago. The government came in and investigated for two years and couldn't find anything and just kept working and working and working trying to find something against us . . . but couldn't find anything. One group after another kept attacking until I thought there wasn't anything left. I felt like a skeleton. I just felt like a skeleton standing in the midst of it . . . like I was picked apart by the vultures.

Oh, I wanted to take off sometimes. The old flesh said, "I don't need this. I can go and sell shoes and make more money than this. I don't have to put up with this."

But I remembered the words of the Lord, "Be thou faithful." And I stood when even my faith was wavering. I stood. And because of that, recently we had the greatest victory moment in our history and a victory parade. An estimated 45,000 people came to help us dedicate the Heritage Auditorium. Our speaker was Oral Roberts and our dedicatory prayer was by Rex Humbard. And friends from all over the world came. I want you to know the Lord was on our side. I didn't do it. I couldn't do it. It was God.

God wants you to survive. He wants you to win the ultimate victory. John 3:16 says, "For God so loved the world, that he gave his only begotten Son, that whosoever believeth in him should not perish, but have everlasting life." God has made a way for us so that we will not perish! God so loved you that He paid the price of His own Son's death so that we could have eternal victory and be freed from our sins.

You simply have to get on God's side and accept His love gift. He's already on your side. He's shown more love to you than the world ever could. If for some reason you haven't gotten on God's side yet, you can right now.

Simply surrender to His love. Simply pray to God and say, "Father, I accept your love gift of Jesus. I know you are on my side; now I want to be on Your side. I want to join forces with You. Forgive me of my sins, and let Your Son Jesus rule my life."

As you pray that prayer to God, He will unite you to Himself. He will place you on the winning side! John 3:17 continues, "For God sent not his Son into the world to condemn the world; but that the world through him might be saved." God did not come in the form of His Son to condemn you and send you to hell. He came to give you victory over sin.

And Jesus does not want you or me to perish in *this* life either. Jesus' death and resurrection made it possible to have victory in this life, too. Whatever the problem is in your life, Jesus' death and resurrection guarantees the fact that you won't perish.

We can be one with God and with each other because of Jesus Christ. As we trust, believe, and move in the name of Jesus, we win together. That's how we survive.

God's goodness overwhelms Jim at the Victory Day celebration at Heritage, U.S.A.

People gather to worship and praise in PTL Club's Heritage Hall (Barn) at its dedication on Victory Day at Heritage, U.S.A., on Labor Day of 1980.

Heritage Hall, where PTL Club broadcasts and seminars take place, blends in nicely with the rest of Heritage, U.S.A.

Completed in December of 1980, PTL Club's World Outreach Center on the grounds of Heritage, U.S.A., now consolidates all the offices and branches of PTL Club so that the ministry may function more efficiently.